FROM PROFIT TO PURPOSE

FROM PROFIT TO PURPOSE

How to Switch from Your Corporate Career
to the Not-For-Profit Sector in Four Easy Steps

STEVE CLIFFORD

FOREWORD BY TIM COSTELLO

ISBN: 978-1-922553-22-5

A catalogue entry for this book is available from the National Library of Australia.

Project management and text design by Publish Central
Cover design by Peter Reardon

Disclaimer
The material in this publication is of the nature of general comment only, and does not represent professional advice. It is not intended to provide specific guidance for particular circumstances and it should not be relied on as the basis for any decision to take action or not take action on any matter which it covers. Readers should obtain professional advice where appropriate, before making any such decision. To the maximum extent permitted by law, the author and publisher disclaim all responsibility and liability to any person, arising directly or indirectly from any person taking or not taking action based on the information in this publication.

To my late father, Bruce, my wife, Amanda,
and Amelia, Robert and Simon –
for encouraging me to be the best I can be.

Contents

Foreword

Steve Clifford was a successful partner in a top-tier legal firm. With 30 years of legal experience his life was successful and his future assured. He was happy, but ...?

On a sabbatical in southern France sitting on a stone fence watching a sunset he recognised something had shifted in him. He didn't want to go back to that comfortable career. Was this just a phase – a mid-life crisis – or the well-documented path of the affluent seeking purpose? Was it merely a vague, if lofty, aspiration to give back?

What began was a long and difficult journey to switch to the not-for-profit (NFP) sector. It wasn't easy and it took 12 months and more than 171 coffees with various people (including me) before he landed an opportunity. He has now served seven years in various NFPs.

Steve has written a gritty handbook for corporate people who often find themselves at such a crossroad. He dispels illusions. He names the blockages. He is honest about his own perceptions on this journey.

I have witnessed these in my hiring of ex-corporate high flyers to NFPs. Many display hubris that says, 'if I have been successful commercially it will be simple to translate that success to manage an NFP'. Really? Yes, your career was successful in making a profit and being well remunerated but now you are being invited into solving global poverty on less than half your former salary. When the goal is so much more complex than a bottom-line result, humility, listening and learning are required.

Or the hubris that says, 'these soft bleeding hearts in the NFP sector desperately need my hard-headed business skills'. Yes, NFPs do benefit from and do need those skills. But because the goal for NFPs is transformational not just transactional, it is infinitely more complex to put those skills to achieving the desired goals.

This is also an excellent handbook for beginners who want to land an NFP career. Steve's insights are gems because they are so practical. This is a workbook with probing questions. I think it is so needed and will be of great benefit to all who work their way through it.

The deeper questions are not ignored. What do you love doing? What are you good at? What causes are you passionate about? How do you like to work? Such questions take us into personal and existential challenges. A life lived well must grapple with these questions.

I am glad that French sunset prompted a personal shift and an inspiring journey. All that has resulted in this valuable book I commend to seekers and colleagues on the journey into their common good.

Tim Costello AO
CEO World Vision Australia 2004–16

Introduction

I was sitting on a stone wall, watching the sun set over the valley below. My wife and I had been living for the last month in the 13th-century hilltop town of Cordes-sur-Ciel, in the south of France. My long service leave was coming to an end and I was mentally preparing myself for our return to Australia, and my life as a corporate lawyer. But as I sat up high on the ramparts, and the sun dipped lower, I felt a strong sense that maybe it was time for a change.

I'd had a 30-year career as a mergers and acquisitions lawyer in one of Australia's top firms, working mainly in Melbourne, but also with stints living and working in New York and Singapore. I loved my life as a lawyer, despite the periods of stress and long hours. I thrived in the fast-paced environment, working with super smart people, and leading teams doing complex and exciting deals.

But as time passed I'd gotten to the stage that I wanted to do something different with my life. I realised it was time to switch my focus to work that was driven by purpose rather than profit, to a life that I could truly say I loved.

Has your job lost its purpose or meaning? Do you have a nagging feeling that you have more to contribute to the community than your present job allows? Could the skills you've developed in the corporate world be better used to help a worthy cause?

If you're asking yourself questions like these, this book is for you.

You only have one life and you want it to be as fulfilling as possible. So maybe you'd like to explore switching to the not-for-profit sector for the next stage of your career.

A few years ago, one of my mentors asked if I'd have a chat with one of their contacts, who was in his early fifties and was a partner in one of the big four accounting firms. Over coffee, he told me that he'd enjoyed his career there, but knew it was time for change and was thinking about the not-for-profit sector. Sound familiar?

Since that meeting, I've had many corporate people contact me to say that they no longer enjoy their job – whether that job be in business, accounting, law, engineering or investment banking. Their financial position is okay and they'd like to use their skills for a more worthwhile cause.

If you've been thinking about making a change, maybe now's the time. If switching sectors is right for you, the sooner you can do it the better. You'll be more open to the new ideas you'll encounter in your transition, and you'll have more time to enjoy your fulfilling new life. The step-by-step guide in this book, taking you through the four key questions for switching, will make it much easier for you to make the transition.

Maybe after reading this book, you'll decide that you'd like to make the switch, but the time is not quite right. You can use this book to help you prepare for your switch, when the time is right.

Or maybe after reading this book, you'll decide that you don't actually want to work in this sector. But you may still want to get more involved – perhaps as a volunteer, supporter or advocate – and feel the joy of being involved in a good cause. You'll still find lots of useful tips and advice throughout this book.

In the following chapter, I outline the work I did to transition to the 'for-purpose' or 'not-for-profit' (NFP) sector. (For simplicity, I use the terms 'not-for-profit' and 'NFP' through the rest of this book, rather than terms such as 'for-purpose organisation', 'social sector' or 'community sector'. Although making a surplus each year is obviously important for the financial sustainability of a not-for-profit organisation, unlike in the corporate sector, making a profit is not the primary objective.)

And I've loved the last eight years – which have included roles as head of Australian operations at Save the Children, chief operating officer at Whitelion, CEO of Doxa Youth Foundation, inaugural CEO of Thrive by Five, the early childhood initiative of Andrew and Nicola Forrest's Minderoo Foundation, and CEO of national food rescue organisation SecondBite.

I've experienced some great successes and some great stuff-ups – such as the time my executive team at Save the Children teamed up with HR to teach me a few tough lessons (a day I still see as the worst in my NFP career – but more on this in chapter 5)! But the stuff-ups are often the best learning experiences. I'm sharing with you everything I have learnt, so your transition can be as smooth as possible. I've also written this book after being inspired by my amazing father who spent his life doing community work – and provided a model of paying back to the community that I've drawn on later in my own life.

Too many people are working in jobs they no longer enjoy or need, chasing a 'life of riches', when transitioning to the NFP sector could give them the rich life they deserve.

This book consolidates all that I have learned from my research and from the roles that I have held since switching sectors. It takes you through the four guiding questions that will inform your switching journey. And it highlights the importance of networking when making your switch, outlining the three starting questions to ask people when you begin your networking research. Finally, I help you pull all the information together, and provide some tips on surviving after you've made the switch.

Throughout the book, I've also included 'Make the switch' sections. These summarise important information and provide practical tips and advice you can use to take action.

The following pages will help you decide whether switching sectors is right for you – and, if it is, provide a step-by-step guide to finding a fulfilling role and a purposeful life in the not-for-profit sector.

See you there!

ONE

Why switch to the not-for-profit sector?

After working for the same company for over 30 years, my father was due to retire at the age of 65. But he was asked to stay on for 'just another year or so' to assist with a project. So he kept working. He finally retired at 68. But soon after his 70th birthday, he died suddenly following heart surgery. He was denied the opportunity to get everything he had hoped for during his lifetime.

My father's experience had a huge impact on me. I was not going to make the same mistake.

Although I was happy to work long hours and loved my 30-odd years as a lawyer in a big city law firm, in the back of my mind, I knew I wanted to learn from Dad's experience; I wanted to leave some time to do what I thought was meaningful. He'd managed to do a lot of purposeful work in parallel to his career, and I tried to follow his example as well as I could on that front. I was the chairman of the charity committee at our law firm, as well as the primary relationship person for the not-for-profits that the firm supported. I always seemed to be dressing up in a tutu, miming Elvis or doing something silly like that for fundraisers, attempting to balance these efforts with my corporate work.

I wanted to make a big difference. But I realised I could only free up the time to do that if I moved away from being a lawyer, once I felt I could financially do that. I waited for a year or two after the youngest of our three kids had finished secondary school, and then I was ready to jump from the law.

During the many years I was in the law, I was lucky enough to be sent to New York in the 1990s, and to Singapore in the 2000s, where I ran our South-East Asian operations. Those times were exciting – being in foreign places, working on challenging deals and building business. Working as a lawyer in Australia was immensely satisfying too – especially winning work and then leading deal teams to carry it out. Other members of my team would often do the detailed work, but I loved bringing in the work and running teams. I delighted in mentoring young lawyers in our law firm, as well as mentoring some young people at charities we worked with.

But in the latter years, a big deal would come in and I no longer felt like celebrating, setting up the team and working weekend after weekend to get the deal done. I couldn't wait to find a younger partner to hand it over to. My priorities had changed from when I started out.

As you get to this stage of your late forties, fifties and early sixties, your parents are likely getting older or may have died. You look at your parents and see their mortality. It makes you think, *Gee, I've only got one life. Am I really living the life that I most want?* Or, as Mary Oliver asked in her poem 'The Summer Day', 'Tell me, what is it you plan to do with your one wild and precious life?'

Fear of the unknown often holds people back from answering this question fully, or acting on their feelings. When people hear that I have left the law, for example, they often say something like, 'I'm not enjoying my job anymore and I think I want to do something more purposeful with my life. But I'm not sure I've got the right skills to make that change or that there will be sufficient challenges. Isn't the charity world just a lot of people standing around and rattling tins on the street corner?'

This fear can mean people choose comfort over switching completely. When I was starting to explore switching, someone said to me, 'You don't have to do that, Steve. You could stay in the corporate world, but just find an area that's got a positive social purpose and bring your own meaning and satisfaction to that.' I received well-meaning suggestions to work for one of the mining companies or banks, which have staff doing excellent work in the environmental, social and governance (ESG) aspects of their businesses, including working with not-for-profits in their communities. Or I was told I could keep working in the corporate world, but spend more of my time and resources on being an advocate or financial supporter for a good cause. Or I could even move to work in the medical or educational area.

Those are all definitely worthy options – but I wasn't interested in them.

I wanted to do something completely different, and get out of the ivory tower. And so I jumped. One week I was on level 32 at 101 Collins Street, Melbourne, and the next I was visiting a 12-year-old child in a youth detention centre outside Launceston, Tasmania. Leading a team doing good on the ground seemed more direct, and way more appealing, than the other options – and making the switch only confirmed this for me.

Switching to the not-for-profit (NFP) sector from the corporate world offers many benefits. The possibility of a more meaningful life is the main one. Most of us want our lives to be purposeful, and work in the NFP sector can nourish your soul and give added purpose to your life. As the saying (often misattributed to Winston Churchill) goes, 'We make a living by what we get; we make a life by what we give.'

> *Most of us want our lives to be purposeful, and work in the NFP sector can nourish your soul and give added purpose to your life.*

Many people hang onto work they no longer find satisfying. They believe they need the money or fear trying something else. I first heard the phrase 'a rich life, not a life of riches' from Paul Ronalds, CEO of Save the Children Australia, in the context of switching sectors. To me, those words held a lot of wisdom. If you feel that a switch to the NFP sector could lead to a richer and more meaningful life for you – along with other benefits, such as making a positive difference – keep reading.

FINDING SATISFYING AND MEANINGFUL WORK

In 2009, when I first started exploring opportunities to do something other than law, I turned to the Birkman Method personality assessment tool, which aims to discover the interests and needs that drive your behaviour.

The tool showed I no longer had much interest in being a lawyer, and that areas such as social service and teaching were now of prime interest for me.

I did the test again in 2014, after I had left the law. In those few years, my interest in law had shrunk from around a 60 per cent rating to something like 30 per cent. The teaching and social work interests were still up around 95 per cent. That confirmed what I already knew: I was no longer interested in being a lawyer. My work as a lawyer had served me well, but I had reached a stage where I wanted a life doing something I found purposeful, enjoyable and meaningful – and law was no longer the answer. That's when I started exploring the not-for-profit sector more deeply.

Michael Traill, a former Macquarie banker and Harvard MBA, made this switch and has given me expert advice and support in my own journey. In *Jumping Ship*, Traill tells how in his forties, after a successful career at Macquarie Bank, known as the 'millionaires' factory', he decided he needed more in his life. He was working on a deal over a weekend and, at the same time, coaching his young son's football team in an important match. He found he was thinking about which position he'd put one boy into on the field, instead of thinking about the multimillion-dollar deal his colleagues were working on back in the office.

That was when he realised that the corporate world wasn't the most meaningful part of his life. And so he found something that was more purposeful – as the inaugural CEO of Social Ventures Australia, an NFP that provides business-type skills, strategic planning and consulting services to other NFPs at a corporate standard and rigour they otherwise could not afford.

Michael loves to refer to a quote from Dr Seuss's *The Lorax*, a book that reminds us that life is about quality rather than quantity:

I meant no harm, I most truly did not. But I had to grow bigger, so bigger I got. I biggered my factory, I biggered my roads, I biggered the wagons, I biggered the loads ... And I biggered my money, which everyone needs.

You can chase the quantity of life, but sometimes it's the quality that's the most important – to do something meaningful and do something with purpose.

In his *Harvard Business Review* article 'Managing Oneself', management consultant guru Peter Drucker argued things have changed since people were happy to retire to leisure, back in the days when work usually involved manual labour. These days, and for people whose careers have been spent more in what Drucker called 'knowledge work', retirement from one career comes less from exhaustion and feeling worn out, and more from boredom. By the time they reach 45, most executives have been doing the same type of work for many years, and are very good at it. However, as Drucker highlighted:

> *You can chase the quantity of life, but sometimes it's the quality that's the most important – to do something meaningful and do something with purpose.*

They are not learning or contributing or deriving challenge and satisfaction from the job. And yet they are still likely to face another 20 or 25 years of work. That is why managing oneself increasingly leads one to begin a second career.

In recent years many people, particularly those in their late forties to early sixties, have asked me about switching. They tell me they are no longer satisfied by the corporate world, but are not yet ready for retirement, and certainly not ready for a life focused on simply relaxing, travelling and playing golf. Others who ask me about switching are younger and only relatively early in their corporate careers, but still feel something is lacking. Each group feels a nagging sense that they could make more of a contribution than they do now, but they are not sure what to do next.

When I arrived at Save the Children to be its first head of Australian operations, it was in the process of merging with an organisation called Good Beginnings. Good Beginnings was a smaller organisation working in a complementary space, with a long-term ambition of building better outcomes for children in vulnerable communities. But as with any merger, bringing two passionate teams together into one organisation had its challenges.

I still remember dealing with the challenges arising from the Good Beginnings staff in the Northern Territory wishing to keep wearing their blue Good Beginnings t-shirts, rather than the red Save the Children ones! But, more significantly, I remember when the penny dropped during one drawn-out meeting, where I helped focus on resolving some of the key merger issues. Many of the issues were ones that had arisen in mergers I'd worked on during my corporate days, and I knew I could add value by suggesting solutions from my past life. I had a strong sense of, 'I can do this, I can actually add value in this new sector' – and it felt so rewarding, when the result was better outcomes for young Australian children and their families, not just corporate shareholders.

Of the hundreds of mergers and acquisitions I have been involved with across all my roles, to this day the Good Beginnings deal was one of the most satisfying.

Make the switch

Ask yourself the following to help you decide whether it might be time to switch to the not-for-profit sector:

- Do you struggle to focus at work?

- Do you feel tired all the time?

- Do you feel reluctant to go to work?

- Do you lack challenges in your job?

- Do you want to learn new stuff but feel as if you know it all?

- Do you want to let go of something that's holding you back?

- Do you feel unsatisfied at the end of your working day or week?

- Do you feel like there's some unfinished business in your life?

The fundamental barriers to living a new purposeful life that you love are your apathy and fear of the unknown. You might ask yourself questions like, 'Do I have the right skills? What cause is important enough to me to do something about it? Will I fit into the sector and relate to the people in it?' How you can address these questions is what the rest of this book is about.

MAKING A POSITIVE DIFFERENCE

When you switch from corporate to NFP, you can make a positive difference to the community and your life will have more purpose. Led by the example of younger generations, more people are seeking meaning in their work. During my law firm years, I was involved in hiring young graduates. While I was focused on asking candidates why we should employ them, they were increasingly asking me what our firm had to offer them as incoming employees – asking about our policies on corporate social responsibility and ESG (environmental, social and governance), for example, or pro bono work. There was a real search for meaning, which I hadn't noticed in my own earlier years as a lawyer. We were just happy to get a job in a good firm and work hard at whatever we were told to do.

This growing search for meaning is being led by the younger generation and, through them, the older generation – people who have been in the workforce for many years – are also starting to ask similar questions. Having a job that paid the bills might have been enough in previous generations. While I'd always wanted to go a step further, and have a job that was challenging as well as paying the bills, the young workers these days are wanting even more, and asking much better questions. They say, 'It's not enough that the job pays the bills and challenges me. Does it fulfil me as a person? Does my work make a positive difference?' And those are brilliant questions to ask.

I am immensely proud that I became a senior partner in one of Australia's top law firms, and that they sent me all over the world to work for them. Although my kids enjoyed hearing my stories from the business world, and appreciated the lifestyle and holidays that came with it, they were much more excited as young adults when I became the CEO of a charity. To me, that shows the importance of knowing your life purpose. Making a positive difference in the community can mean a lot more than just having a job that pays the bills.

When I decided to leave the law, one of my first steps was to meet with players in the NFP sector to see whether a purposeful role might be found for me in that sector. Over a 12-month period, I had 171 coffees with senior NFP leaders. (Don't worry – with the help of this book, you won't have to meet with that many people!) During this 'due diligence' period, I met many who reassured me that some of my transferable corporate skills and rigour were needed in the NFP sector. And not just the skills I brought from my background were needed. Expertise was also needed in finance, HR, IT and so on.

In Stephen Covey's *The 7 Habits of Highly Effective People*, he talks about sitting in a church, with the light streaming through stained glass windows. Lovely organ music is being played. He looks down at the order of service and he realises it's his own funeral. The order of service has four headings. One eulogy is from the family, one from friends, one from business associates and one from a community organisation. Covey asks, 'What do we want people to say at our funeral?' When I read that chapter, it was like a chill down my spine. I realised I didn't really have anyone who'd be able to say very much about my contribution to any community organisation, even though I thought that was an important area of my life. Covey sets out a challenge to ensure that we're living a life that will result in the funeral we'd like to see.

Make the switch

Make a list of the benefits you currently derive from your work, with a score out of ten showing how important each one is to you. For example, you may score earning a good salary as 4/10, keeping your partner happy as 8/10 and making a difference as 7/10.

Give yourself inspiration. Think about the people you know who've gained purpose in their life by contributing to their community. In my case, I had a model in my father. Although he didn't have much time between retirement and his death, while he was still working, he was very involved in community work. The school where he was on the school council for decades has a Clifford House, and a memorial garden is named after him at the local church where he served. He set up the local Probus Club and they established an annual oration in his memory. Dad never received an Australia Day award. But when he died, the church was packed.

DON'T WAIT TOO LONG

I spent my thirties and forties working hard to establish a career and earn enough to pay the costs of raising a family, having memorable holidays and providing for our later years.

What most of us run out of is time, not money.

But as I moved from my forties to my fifties, I started to worry that I would run out of time, not money – time to do what I wanted beyond working as a lawyer. What most of us run out of is time, not money. If you can make the financial aspects work, it's better to be proactive rather than reactive and not waste precious years in work that you find unfulfilling.

Part of my thinking was influenced by the life-changing book *Twenty Good Summers* by New Zealand financial adviser Martin Hawes, which I read during my long service leave in 2013. Hawes points out that, although we may live for many years beyond 70, the 20 years from 50 to 70 are the best ones to get on and do the things that we have always wanted to do (which in Hawes's case included climbing, doing seminars, biking and skiing). You might be thinking about making a switch even earlier than 50.

Years earlier, I had read another thought-provoking book: *Halftime* by Bob Buford. Buford uses the metaphor of a football game to argue that, as we approach our mid-forties, we should all take a half-time pause and look for new horizons and new challenges. He writes,

> Instead of giving up and settling for life on its own terms, you are ready ... to move from success to significance – to write your own epitaph – daring to believe that what you ultimately leave behind will be more important than you could have achieved in the first half of your life.

Both authors support the view that time becomes increasingly precious as we approach the latter years of our working life. Again – most of us will run out of time, not money.

And evidence supports the argument that time is becoming increasingly scarce compared to our incomes. Research by Professor Daniel S. Hamermesh, for example, shows that, whereas real incomes (measured as GDP per capita) almost tripled in Australia from 1960 to 2010, the increase in life expectancy only increased by 15 per cent. In his article 'The time of our lives', Hamermesh asks, 'Why do people worry so much about their incomes and so little about how they spend their time?' Given those figures, it makes sense for us to focus on how we spend our time, rather than worrying about money!

Many people who have spent a lifetime in the corporate world feel burnt out or ready for the slower pace of retirement. But they may also wonder what else life could hold for them; they may still want to 'give back' to their community. If you are like me, that 'giving back' may be in the form of a paid role. (We need to be careful about using words such as 'give back' because we don't want to be seen as do-gooders who fly in briefly with our corporate jet pack, wave our magic corporate wand, and then disappear.) But I had a strong sense that I wasn't only on the planet to help big corporates finalise big deals and lock in big profits.

I knew that the NFP sector was under-resourced, that there was never enough money or resources to deal with all the needs of the people falling between the cracks – and to deal with issues such as poverty, youth justice, homelessness and Indigenous parity. And yet at the same time I felt that people like me in the corporate sector had skills and experience that might be useful to the overburdened charities doing their work. But would the people working in the charities want people from the corporate sector to come and work with them?

Once I worked with a young lawyer who had a big social conscience. He would have been very successful in the law, but he decided early on that he wanted to move to the NFP sector. He is still working in that sector. I bumped into him recently at the Garma Festival of Traditional Cultures (held in north-east Arnhem Land in the Northern Territory, Australia) and was impressed with how he had brought to the sector his corporate learning and the rigour of his law degree and a few years' training. I know he will really have a huge impact in the NFP sector. And his journey is a great reminder that you can choose to switch in your early career years, not just later on.

So it's not just people who are approaching the end of their careers who can move into the sector. Making the switch is not just about retirement or burnout. It's about wanting to make more of a contribution than you are now. Don't wait until you're too old. You might be ready to switch very early on from a corporate career, with whatever skills you have built by then. The suggestions in this book will help at that stage as well.

> *Making the switch is not just about retirement or burnout. It's about wanting to make more of a contribution than you are now. Don't wait until you're too old.*

People tell me they're unsure about the timing and don't want to leave the corporate world too early. The process outlined in this book should help you deal with those concerns and decide if and when the time is right.

Make the switch

Even if you're not burned out and not ready for retirement, you can ask yourself whether you would like your life to have more significance.

Write a list of the pros and cons for switching, including the financial aspects. Then talk to those close to you – perhaps your partner and/or your children and your close friends. But be careful when you talk to people who know you in your existing role and make sure they don't close down your thinking. When senior people talk to others in the corporate world and say, 'Oh, I'm thinking about switching to become a leader in the not-for-profit world', the cursory response could be, 'Oh, no. You're so good where you are. If you feel like a change, why don't you just try something different at the company you're already at?'

What are you looking forward to, work-wise? What would you like to learn? What strengths would you like to use more? And what does success mean to you? Take some time away from the stress of everyday life and talk about those issues with people who know you.

EXTENDING YOUR WORKING LIFE

Despite the laws against age discrimination, many people in their fifties are let go by their company because of their age. But it's way too young to retire. And we're living longer, which means even retiring in your sixties can leave a lot of time to fill after leaving the workforce. For both reasons, a more gratifying solution might be an 'encore' career in the NFP sector.

An alternative to a paid role is to be an unpaid volunteer, which means at least you have the satisfaction of contributing positively to society. For years, many people have gone down that track. But the overall point of this book is that you may prefer to try for a paid gig and really commit yourself to the sector. This is separate from offering skilled volunteering services to get your foot in the door, which I talk about in chapter 9.

In Australia, many older people feel underutilised and would like to work for longer. In 2019, Dr Kay Patterson AO, the Age Discrimination Commissioner, pointed out that significant economic benefits for the country come from recruiting and retaining older workers. Doing so also creates a great opportunity for skilled corporates who have contributed in the business world to switch to a more meaningful way of giving back – rather than just heading to the golf course or doing overseas travel.

The trouble is, you can't see many other switchers just at the moment. But I've done it. It's been terrific – most of the time! I'm learning more about the sector, being useful and still have a lot of energy. I can see myself doing this for many more years than I would have considered working as a lawyer.

In the business world, I often held corporate networking lunches with clients from different sectors. I loved learning about their businesses and challenges, and about the individuals themselves. When I stopped being a lawyer, one of my clients invited me back to one of their own similar networking lunches. At the end of this particular lunch, as we were walking to the lift, I spoke to one fellow who was from a headhunting firm. I said, 'I hope you don't think I'm rude for asking, Simon, but you seem a couple of years older than the others. Can you tell me how old you are?'

He replied, 'I'm 77, Steve.' He saw the surprise in my face and said, 'You didn't think I was that old, did you?'

'No,' I said, 'but I'm really impressed. Can you tell me a little about what's going on?'

He said, 'Well, I retired at 65. I spent a year or two at home reading the paper, driving my wife crazy and finding that all of my mates were just playing golf. I felt like I was out of the loop of important discussions and I was finding it boring. I went back to my former employer and said, "Can I just have a small office, come in and be available as a resource? You don't have to pay me, but I'd quite like an office." To cut a long story short, I've been doing that for ten years and I'm sure it's a win–win for me and the organisation.

And it's been a new lease of life for me.' This conversation just highlighted to me the value that could have been lost if this fellow, with his extraordinary experience in the executive recruitment world, had spent all his time with his wife and his golf mates.

As demographer Bernard Salt wrote in the article 'Why we need to reimagine the retirement years':

> If life expectancy continues to improve, the retirement years need to be reimagined. The pandemic-inspired older-worker surge is part of a bigger movement in which the working life is extended for those who, by choice, refuse to retire.

If you doubt your ability to extend your life beyond retirement, you will find many positive ideas in this book to minimise those feelings. Taking a clear look at your transferable skills is key. They may apply in other areas, including the NFP world.

Though I have loved the change and found it really invigorating, moving to the NFP sector isn't for everyone. Some people prefer to step down into a smaller organisation in the same sector or find a volunteer role that uses some of their skills.

Make the switch

From the people you know, reflect on those who worked to 65 or beyond in the same career, and those (there may not be many) who retired before 65 or changed careers. If you were to rate their individual happiness out of ten, what score would you give them? This exercise may help you get some perspective about what future direction might work best for you.

I did this exercise (during lots of post-sailing chats over the years) with the 60- to 80-year-old group at the yacht club bar. It confirmed to me the importance at that stage of life of having a purpose that means a lot to you – and that this purpose was often tied to some sort of contribution to the community. Those whose purpose involved a paid role seemed particularly happy, and felt more valued. Many I spoke to had not really enjoyed the latter working years, when they were hanging out for retirement.

WRAP UP

Rather than being trapped in a corporate career that's bringing less and less joy, an alternative option can bring increased purpose and meaning to your life – and still bring a salary. And you don't need to wait until you are old or approaching retirement. Wanting to switch is a feeling, not an age.

As you explore switching through this book, at times you may feel it's all just too hard. I explore challenges such as going outside your comfort zone, and dealing with emotional and financial challenges, a lack of resources and support, and stakeholder complexity. Why bother taking on all these challenges? Because that's part of the adventure, right? And because leaving our comfort zone occasionally is good, and the complexity is what makes the sector so interesting. I love taking on a challenge – and succeeding. If you understand these challenges in advance, are willing to do the work and use your corporate skills in different ways, you can switch – and enjoy the benefits of a more meaningful life. How good would that be?

You can expect to encounter internal and external resistance to your transition – including colleagues feeling threatened, ageism, and cynicism towards corporate refugees. Overcoming this resistance will be easier if you can understand the sector differences, find NFP mentors and supporters, and maintain a positive outlook. Through the inevitable ups and downs on your switching journey, keep your eye on the prize – a new life filled with purposeful work, doing what you love doing.

The next chapter will help you understand what the sector differences are in advance, so you can be ready for them.

TWO

Not-for-profit versus the corporate world

In my first week as chief operating officer at youth charity Whitelion, the Victorian state manager invited me to a meeting. About 24 young people were in the room, many with tattoos and body piercings. Wild hairdos abounded, coloured and razor-clipped. I whispered to the manager, 'Are these the people we work with? Our clients?'

He replied, 'No, Steve. This is your staff.' And so I learnt another lesson about how different my new sector would be from my old business world. They were fantastic staff – but very different from the young law graduates in their suits.

To make the switch successfully, you need to step into the not-for-profit (NFP) world with an understanding of the differences between the two sectors.

In the corporate world, we often have lots of resources and lots of staff to help us do our jobs – including personal assistants, IT help desk personnel, and people providing photocopying and delivery services. In the NFP world, resources are much scarcer. I'd been warned about that, and that I would have to be a lot more self-sufficient. Someone had suggested that I should learn how to change a toner cartridge before I left the sheltered workshop of the big law firm. Good advice – and I'm an expert now!

Understanding different cultures before you move sectors is important too. In one of my NFP leadership roles, I found out a deadline was about to pass that afternoon for a significant grant application. The staff member who was responsible for submitting the grant application was away sick. I wondered whether that staff member had already got the application in, so I did what I would have done at any corporate role when I had an important question – I phoned the staff member on their mobile. It turned out the application had not been properly submitted and we were running out of time that day. I was not happy about the situation, or about having to put aside other things to urgently fix the situation. And the staff member was not happy that I had disturbed them at home on their sick day with an angry phone call, and subsequently made an internal complaint. It was a fascinating experience for me – something that would have just been a given in the corporate world, but that created significant angst in the NFP world.

In this chapter, I discuss how to achieve success in the NFP sector, where passion and commitment are more important than skills. I also outline how leaders need to use their vision to capture the hearts and minds of the staff. Compared to the corporate world, the typical NFP CEO has far less authority and control. Titular and autocratic leadership just don't work here – building relationships and being patient does.

I then look at how more listening and less talking is necessary to bring people along in the NFP sector and have them follow your vision. When you set a strategic goal or you've got your plan for the year, sitting down with them, listening to their concerns and helping to solve their problems will help bring your staff along with you – which involves a lot of listening. I also talk about keeping your focus on collaboration rather than competition. Collaboration can be a great way of achieving outcomes in the NFP sector where you have only limited resources. And, finally, I discuss how the NFP sector has more complexity than the corporate world, especially regarding regulations, stakeholders and resourcing.

In their McKinsey article, 'What you don't know about managing nonprofits – and why it matters', authors Les Silverman and Lynn Taliento (co-founders of McKinsey & Company's Global Nonprofit Practice) quoted some experts in this area of transition. Bill Novelli, CEO of US interest group AARP and former head of CARE, told them succeeding in the non-profit world was harder than in the corporate world, firstly because the goals are more complex and harder to achieve.

While acknowledging competing in sectors such as consumer goods, electronics or finance was still hard, Novelli argued,

> It's harder to achieve goals in the nonprofit world because these goals tend to be behavioural. If you set out to do something about breast cancer in this country, or about Social Security solvency, it's a hell of a lot harder to pull that off. It's also harder to measure.

The article makes an interesting point – it is more complicated to succeed in the NFP world because of those behavioural goals. In this sector, you're not just selling more widgets, and the goals you're seeking to meet are harder to measure. In other words, it's not just about the profit.

Another point worth making is that the NFP sector has a huge variety of organisations, just as there are in the business world. This variety runs from small, community-based volunteer-run NFPs to large, complex organisations such as Mission Australia or Save the Children. How they operate, and whether they are the right fit for you, will depend on your particular circumstances. I have tried to draw some general similarities to guide your thinking – and the importance of passion is one common theme.

Many people working in the NFP sector are guided by their heart rather than their head. To be compassionate about the people you are serving is a wonderful thing, but sometimes it can be problematic. I found that although a board and CEO may have encouraged me to bring my corporate expertise into their organisations, sometimes the frontline staff struggled with my approach. A common example was staff wanting to continue a favourite program even though it had lost funding or was not achieving the expected outcomes. People from the corporate world may be less emotional, with a background based on dollar-led decisions. Understanding differences like these will put you in a better position to take the best of both approaches. The business world's focus on the profit motive can lead some NFP staff to be cynical about 'corporate refugees' and view them as shallow do-gooders. That might be one reason switchers are so scarce.

PASSION AND COMMITMENT ARE VITAL

An oft-cited adage in the NFP sector (based on a saying by US President Theodore Roosevelt) is, 'We don't care what you know, until we know you care.'

To be able to work well with others who are already in the sector, you need to be able to communicate your passion and commitment to them. Having a passion for the cause is the key difference between the corporate sector and the NFP sector. Your own passion is important, but so is understanding what is most important to your team. What are their drivers? If you don't understand this about your colleagues, you won't be as effective in bringing along your team. Salaries aren't as high in this sector, partly because people are willing to accept lower pay if they feel they are working for a meaningful cause. That's why passion and commitment are so important, giving you and your colleagues a reason to go to work beyond just the pay cheque.

'We don't care what you know, until we know you care.'

The NFP sector has been criticised in the past for being satisfied with the process, rather than focusing on the outcomes for the clients and beneficiaries. An attitude can develop of 'I've devoted my life to helping people, what more do you want?'

Many of my NFP mentors told me that they were motivated to break the status quo, to really 'Move the dial', and would often tell me how they first got involved in their organisation. One example is Mark Watt, co-founder and former CEO of Whitelion (and also a longstanding friend and mentor of mine). Mark was seeing young people face a revolving door at Parkville Youth Justice Centre (in Melbourne), and then go on to a lifetime in and out of adult prison. He wanted to break this cycle and that's why he set up Whitelion. Whenever he spoke with funders or staff, Mark would mention some recent poignant incident involving a young person, which would touch the heart (and wallet) of each listener. His passion showed through as he spoke and it was very powerful. He was the CEO for 20 years, so if that doesn't show a passion and commitment to that cause, then I don't know what does.

My own experiences also confirmed the truth of this proposition. With new contacts or teams I was working with, I'd often start by telling them about the impact my father's community work had on me from an early age, followed by my pro bono and mentoring work while in the business world, and then stories of various clients that really stirred my emotions.

When I was working at Whitelion as chief operating officer, I went to Tasmania to catch up with my state manager. The organisation works with youth at risk, particularly working with young people in juvenile detention situations. My manager said, 'I'm going to meet one of our clients this afternoon. Would you like to come along?' I'm a curious person so I said yes. After a comprehensive identification process at the entrance to the youth detention centre, and going through several locked doors, I was inside Ashley Youth Detention Centre (near Deloraine in the north of Tasmania).

The young fellow with whom my colleagues were working came from a traumatic background. He had experienced a lot of issues with family violence – his father was in jail, his mother was on drugs. He just had no moral compass as to what was right and wrong. He ended up killing someone and, by 12 years of age, was in youth detention.

I saw my state manager's compassion and care towards this young person, and the experience was an eye opener for me in regards to the needs of a part of the community I rarely saw. I thought, *If I can make any contribution of my time to a young person like this, this is worthwhile.* I bonded with him and we had a lovely chat. On his left forearm he had inked himself a rough tattoo that read 'Mum'. I felt that deep down he had a lot of good in him, but he'd had such a terrible life.

One reason that NFP staff are willing to work for salaries that are lower than their corporate equivalents is the satisfaction derived from working towards a cause that is important to them. On the other side of the coin, maybe people wouldn't work in the corporate sector, in a job they don't like very much, if they weren't earning those larger amounts of money.

Make the switch

Reflect on your past activities while in the corporate world and make a list of times where you've been willing to do something without getting anything back – for example, organising an office fundraiser, sitting on a tennis club committee, volunteering for charity, fundraising for a new club building, or maybe providing some skilled pro bono work for a charity. That may give some indication of your own passion and commitment. Connect to your sense of value around delivering a service when it's not related to money.

LEADERS NEED TO WIN HEARTS AND MINDS

Compared to the corporate world, the typical NFP CEO has less authority and control. Another saying from the sector is based on an African proverb: 'If you want to go fast, go alone. If you want to go far, go together.'

As a business person, you may be used to a system where a leader automatically earns some measure of respect – simply because they are the boss. I have never seen an NFP CEO who has succeeded by simply relying on their position. I've seen this happen in the business world, but never in the NFP world. Maybe that's another reason it's not very common to have someone come from the business world into the NFP world as a leader.

To succeed as a leader in the NFP sector, you will need to demonstrate your passion and your vision, and build trust in order to bring your staff along on the journey with you. Your staff (and boss) will also want to see a willingness to work hard on the passion you share with them, as well as humility and an openness to learn.

In the article I quoted earlier in this chapter ('What you don't know about managing nonprofits – and why it matters'), authors Les Silverman and Lynn Taliento also quote Reynold Levy, former CEO of Lincoln Centre for the

To succeed as a leader in the NFP sector, you will need to demonstrate your passion and your vision, and build trust in order to bring your staff along on the journey with you.

Performing Arts, who had served formerly as an executive at AT&T. Levy said, 'In the world of nonprofits deference to the CEO is rare. You really need to earn that respect. It doesn't come by virtue of your title.'

Doxa Youth Foundation is a 50-year-old organisation that supports children from low socioeconomic backgrounds in Victoria, through primary school camps, secondary school coaching and cadetships for tertiary study and into the workforce.

When I started at Doxa as CEO, it was important to me to create a vision for the team to follow, to help lift their performance and impact. Because I had been a donor and a mentor to some of the Doxa cadets for many years before I took the job, I had a head start in having the Doxa staff listen to me, and earning their trust. They could see that I was already committed to the cause and that I shared their passion and commitment.

Whitelion's Mark Watt provides another example. At every annual conference with his state managers, Mark would put up a graph showing where the funding gaps were. He had a clever way of showing his own commitment by saying, 'I've put myself down for as many dollars as I can, and you guys have done a great job, but all of us need to step up a little bit further. Who's going to volunteer to add a couple of dollars to their fundraising budget for the year so we can fill the gap?' That appealed to their better natures and to come along with his vision. This struck me as being quite different from the corporate world where your budgets are often just imposed by the CEO – although sometimes after strong debate!

This doesn't mean that NFP CEOs don't also need a tough side. Tough decisions still have to be made in the NFP sector – for example, having to close programs or terminate staff. But in that situation, it's much more important to explain the rationale and to bring the other staff along with you.

When I first arrived at one NFP, I felt one staff member didn't share the culture I was hoping to engender. The employee talked about people behind their backs and their work ethic wasn't as strong as I wanted. I wanted the team to be working hard, and as a unified team. Quite early on, I dismissed this person – and the interesting part was the number of people who said, 'We were hoping someone would do that; that person's been a negative influence for too long.'

NFP leaders are aware that sometimes they need a slightly tougher hand, and that they can't afford to be too soft. But it is a tricky line to draw because most people in the NFP world are caring people. We're helping people in the community who we know need a hand. When you decide to terminate someone, resistance can come from the other staff.

You may not be familiar with this type of leadership. It takes practice. You need to swallow your frustration, at least until staff and stakeholders have developed their trust in you, because you'll spend way more time listening to people and capturing their hearts and minds than you used to. You cannot bring them along with you by saying, 'We'll do it this way because I'm the boss.'

In their McKinsey article, Les Silverman and Lynn Taliento also quote NFP leader (and former US Ambassador) Philip Lader, who says leading non-profits is similar in some ways to being an ambassador:

There you are at the helm of the great ship, with everyone scurrying about. Only after about four months of steering the wheel do you realise that it's not connected to the rudder. Everyone is saluting you and saying, 'Aye aye', as they then go below to steer the ship themselves. In many nonprofits, that genuinely is the case.

This 'dissipated authority' is relatively common in the NFP sector. It reminds me of the story of the hospital cleaner who kept moving the pictures on the walls of the hospital rooms. Her boss told her not to – but she was more interested in keeping 'her customers' happy with the choice of art work. You think you're the boss and people are saying yes, yes, yes, but they won't actually do anything you want until you've won them over.

> *You think you're the boss and people are saying yes, yes, yes, but they won't actually do anything you want until you've won them over.*

Make the switch

Reflect on your own leadership style and be aware that you may have to soften your approach. Don't be soft about making tough decisions but implement them in a way that respects and acknowledges different perspectives.

Which leaders have you worked with who have the ability to have you walking over broken glass for them, and not just because they're your boss? Of course, good leaders in the corporate world need to capture the hearts and minds of their staff to be successful. But, ultimately, they have the choice of saying, 'I'm your boss. Just do it.' It's not as easy to rely on that titular authority in the NFP world.

MORE LISTENING AND LESS TALKING

The dissipated authority model I talk about in the previous section shows that you'll need good listening skills to be effective. Part of the reason that NFP leaders begin with less authority than their corporate equivalents is they have to take into account the interests of so many stakeholders. This can make them feel like they'll never get to make a decision. Les Silverman and Lynn Taliento highlight this in their article as well, with one CEO Bill Novelli noting the 'eternal consensus building' slows down not only decision-making but also action. He quotes a consultant brought in to one NFP as saying, 'Around here it's, "ready, aim, aim, aim."'

People in the NFP sector place a high value on interpersonal skills. They prefer to explore issues through sufficient discussion – whether this is starting or stopping a client program, or changing strategic direction – rather than just being told to implement the CEO's directive memo at the start of business next week. And this listening can also apply at board level, not just with your staff. In the corporate world, the goal of most board members is to achieve their shareholders' financial objectives for the company, usually to maximise profits. But in the NFP sector, even board members may come with different goals and agendas. That can make it more complex for a CEO. Ideally, the board members will listen to each other to find and work towards a common goal. But if they don't, as CEO you may need to build and use your interpersonal skills to make progress.

This idea of listening, listening, listening is new to a lot of us. In 'Making executive transitions work' (published in *Social Ventures Australia Quarterly*) the authors interviewed six CEOs in the NFP sector, some who had come from the corporate world and some who hadn't, about what's important for a successful transition. As the authors note, 'The social purpose environment is also, somewhat famously, more people-centric and as a result requires stronger interpersonal skills and emotional intelligence.' Catherine Yeomans, then CEO of Mission Australia, added,

> It was explained to me very early on by a senior person in our organisation ... that we are a human services organisation, we are a people organisation. Everything that we do needs to be spoken about and explained through the lens of the people we work with (our clients) and our staff.

Note the need to talk through everything, and to do so from the clients' perspective.

When I was brought in as CEO of food rescue organisation SecondBite, it was clear that the internal culture needed a lot of work. Rather than just using change management skills developed in prior roles to simply launch into 'fix it' mode, I spent much of the first two months just meeting with and listening to as many staff from around the country as I could – from the warehouse staff and truck drivers, through to the leadership team. Only then did I feel that I had started to build sufficient trust, and sufficient understanding of the staff's views, to get to work on changing the organisation's culture.

You may be asking, 'How is anything achieved if you sit around all day, listening and listening to every member of your team?' But once your team feels that they have been heard and they have started to build trust in you, you won't need to spend quite as much time listening at every point. You will find an equilibrium. After all, you have been brought in to lead, not just to listen.

On some occasions, saying what you have to say without spending too much time listening will be appropriate. For example, at one organisation a theft by our bookkeeper was discovered. The end result was that I promptly let that person go, with compassion but no team discussion.

Make the switch

Start practising your listening skills. Good listening skills don't come naturally to everyone, and you might have succeeded in the corporate world without yours being too good. Developing these skills might feel frustrating or a little too touchy feely. But the best way to start practising is by mirroring back to the other person what you think they said. Your partner might find this is useful too – mine certainly told me to do more of it! Practice makes perfect.

COLLABORATION NOT COMPETITION

Collaboration is often the primary mode of achieving outcomes in the NFP sector, due to limited resources. In the NFP context, collaboration usually means working with another NFP or other party on a joint project. The objective is to achieve, in a situation of limited funding or other resources, a better outcome jointly than you would have had working separately.

Although collaboration in the NFP context is often used to refer to collaboration between NFP providers, it can also be between service providers and philanthropic organisations, or with corporates. Each of those organisations would effectively be worse off in the absence of collaboration, not forgetting the clients who are benefiting from all this work.

Collaboration may not be something you need in the corporate world – especially if you're a tough litigation lawyer like some of my former partners. The corporate world thrives on competition not collaboration. However, in the NFP world being able to collaborate is an important skill. When Doxa collaborated with the Centre for Multicultural Youth to combine our respective expertise, for example, we applied jointly to fund a new program to help young people from refugee backgrounds to transition into the workforce. Doxa's 20-year experience running its cadetship program gave it expertise in assisting young people into the workforce.

The corporate world thrives on competition not collaboration. However, in the NFP world being able to collaborate is an important skill.

And the Centre for Multicultural Youth added a new dimension with their expertise in supporting young people facing a variety of cultural issues. It was a wonderful example of two organisations coming together – neither organisation would have received the funding and the program wouldn't have happened without the other organisation's input.

Another example is the collaboration between Whitelion and the Reach Foundation to provide mentoring programs to disadvantaged youth. The Reach Foundation was set up about 25 years ago by Jimmy Stynes of the Melbourne Football Club. It's a youth-run organisation that provides workshops to help young people support each other and learn from their own experiences to get through tough times in life. The joint RAMP programs blended the two groups so that Whitelion youth at risk were involved, as well as the Reach young people from more mainstream backgrounds.

Particularly if you're used to the cut and thrust of the corporate world as I was, you might find it interesting to see how NFPs can work together to achieve the required outcomes. Examples like the RAMP program, and the joint Doxa and Centre for Multicultural Youth program, are proof that you can collaborate in this sector. It doesn't happen very well in the corporate world, but it certainly does in the NFP sector. In fact, when you've got limited resources, finding innovative ways to help the people that your organisation is working to help is crucial.

Of course, it's not always sweetness and light – a tension can exist between collaboration and competition. Collaboration doesn't always work as well as it should, or doesn't work at all – for example, your organisation may be competing with a similar service provider for a fixed grant amount. Some foundations, having seen that behaviour, now encourage the NFPs to collaborate if they want to receive any funds. But, at times, NFPs do need to be competitive because of the way the funding is set up. They have no choice. I wouldn't suggest anyone throw away their 'How to be a tough competitor' manual just yet. But, generally, collaboration is more pervasive than competition.

Collaboration is also important internally within your organisation. Earlier in this chapter, I talk about bringing a team along with your vision. Each organisation has several divisions: accounts, fundraising, programs, operations and so on. Those departments working collaboratively was important for me. For example, with the fundraisers, going out and asking for money or agreeing to funding for a new program is pointless if our operations and programs people can't deliver. Similarly, if our operations and programs people have a great idea, they need to explain this to the fundraising people so they can go out and pitch it. These are all forms of internal collaboration.

Make the switch

Start to build up your NFP network and your list of potential collaborators will grow. (I discuss networking in chapter 8.)

Coming from a corporate background, you may have a cynical or untrusting starting point when exploring a possible collaboration. Let that go. One of your transferable skills from the business world is likely to be your ability to be strategic, possibly in the areas of joint ventures, mergers and partnerships. Use those skills in the NFP sector to ensure you've got the right partner organisations and to develop a collaboration with mutual benefits.

You being able to lead by example and make the first concession will help engender a spirit of trust where people say, 'Well, they're willing to give up something, I could give something too.' Before you know it, you're collaborating for a joint benefit.

DEALING WITH EXTRA COMPLEXITY

More complexity exists in the NFP sector, especially with respect to regulations, stakeholders and resourcing. But that's what makes it fun!

The corporate sector is generally much easier and less complex than the NFP sector. The good news is this complexity will give you a challenge.

Being forewarned of this complexity will help you prepare for it without becoming disheartened. Coming from my background, I thought that working in the sector would be pretty straightforward. See the need. Get the money. Deliver the service. Simple. But it's not like that. In fact, the corporate sector is generally much easier and less complex than the NFP sector. The good news is this complexity will give you a challenge. As one mentor said to me, 'Don't take a job with a charity that's doing well. Pick one that has challenges and complexity – that's where you can add most value.'

In 'Making executive transitions work', the authors talk about the challenge for large NFP organisations to manage scale combined with complexity. Catherine Yeomans says, 'At Mission Australia there's 3800 staff, 500 different contracts, and properties right across Australia. Some commercial people have transferable experience that is broader and deeper than we need. So long as the fit and commitment is right we get more bang for our buck.'

When I was doing my due diligence, Tim Costello, then CEO of World Vision, said to me, 'Don't think working in the sector will be easy for you just because of all your experience with multimillion-dollar deals. The NFP sector is more complex than you think.' How right he was.

As Dr Catherine Brown, OAM, notes in *Great Foundations*, many reasons exist for the sector's complexity. These include:

- diverse income sources, with disparate reporting and accountability requirements, and no integrated federal/state framework (although Sue Woodward, AM, at Justice Connect is doing a great job to improve that situation)

- complex taxation regulation through the *Income Tax Assessment Act*

- difficulties in tackling social, educational, cultural, health and environmental problems

- salaries that are usually below other sectors, so staff expect other non-financial rewards

- board members usually not being paid (and in challenging times board and management roles can become blurred)

- pressure from funders for innovation or at least continual improvement

- constant changes by the state and federal governments in the public policy environment.

In this world of diffused governance, the stakeholders you're likely to encounter include regulators, government staff and elected representatives, funders, internal staff, volunteers, founders, board members, other NFP workers and the public. All of these stakeholders can see themselves as your boss – and bringing them along with you on major decisions can be challenging, if not exhausting. In *Good to Great and the Social Sectors*, author Jim Collins identifies a specific form of (Level 5) leadership to succeed in the social sector. Collins describes these Level 5 leaders as 'incredibly ambitious', but stresses 'their ambition is first and foremost for the cause, for the organization and its purpose, not themselves'. By comparison, a corporate CEO can focus on dealing with their board and their staff, with a clear objective to maximise profits.

Public interest in charities raises an extra complexity. If you're running a private business and something goes wrong, as long as you're not breaking the law it can be dealt with quietly behind closed doors. But with NFPs, particularly the ones receiving external funding, if anything goes wrong it can be splashed everywhere in the headlines. NFPs trade on trust with the public. And if something goes wrong and they lose that trust, they have to work particularly hard to get it back. Public money and taxpayer funds are often involved in NFPs and so the public applies a high standard.

Perhaps you remember some examples of when this trust was lost. Oxfam, for example, had issues in their Haiti office with people who behaved badly, and that affected the whole organisation. Sometimes, the reduction in trust also affects other NFPs. When the Shane Warne Foundation was in the media, for example, with reports that high salaries had been paid to family members, many of us in the sector were grilled for weeks. Stakeholders started asking, 'Are you NFP guys all tickling the till?' Well, no, but trust has been lost and so needed to be rebuilt.

However, the complexities go beyond merely maintaining a high degree of public trust. NFPs need to be on top of regulations about financial reports, working with children, OH&S, tax deductibility and deductible gift recipient status. For a charity that has only a dozen staff, how are they going to find their way through all that?

Never having enough money or resources causes more complexity. In a small organisation, you may never be quite sure whether you will have enough money to pay the salaries for the next month. The complexity of their operational, regulatory and cultural environment also adds many constraints and rising costs for NFPs, which means they have little in reserves to fall back on. Unlike a corporate, they cannot just raise capital by taking on debt or issuing shares. The environment can be very tough and very complex.

Some parts of the NFP sector are more complex than others; for example, the aged care sector, or working with vulnerable young people (such as at Doxa, where we worked with young people on overnight camps and high ropes courses), are inherently complex.

Make the switch

Reflect on which skills from your past corporate life may be useful in dealing with the complexity you'll encounter in the NFP sector. When have you had to work your way through excessive bureaucracy and red tape? The skills you used then will be useful as you switch.

Think about your own leadership style, and how you may need to adapt it to succeed with such complexity and disparate stakeholders.

You might need to upscale your knowledge and skill levels in some of these areas of complexity – for example, through completing a course of external study.

And remember – if you like a challenge and want to make a difference, this complexity could be good news for you!

WRAP UP

You now have a better understanding of the key differences between the corporate and the NFP sectors, which will help you as you make your transition.

Be prepared to communicate your passion to a potentially cynical and resistant NFP sector. And be ready to adapt to a different leadership style that involves more listening and collaboration. Differences do exist between these sectors – but don't worry, you'll become familiar with them. This is just the start. Don't let these differences undermine your confidence.

Four guiding questions can help with your switching journey – and you'll find out what they are in the next chapter.

THREE

Four keys to a successful switch

This chapter provides a framework of four guiding questions. Of all the questions I've asked, I found these four to be the most helpful in my journey. The path from a corporate career to a not-for-profit (NFP) career is not well worn. Asking these questions of myself, and of my NFP sector net-

> *You will need to battle inertia. How to spend your life is a big question and changing what you've perhaps been doing for a long time isn't easy.*

work as I grew it, gave me confidence that I did have something worthwhile to bring to the sector while also helping me find the best fit. These questions will save you a lot of time.

I have met many candidates who talk of how much they'd like to move to a fulfilling NFP role, but never get past thinking and talking to actually doing the work and asking the important questions.

You will need to battle inertia. How to spend your life is a big question and changing what you've perhaps been doing for a long time isn't easy. Finding out what you like, which is a variation of how you want to spend your life, can be difficult too.

I provide an overview of each question in this chapter, and then discuss each in more detail in the chapters that follow.

WHAT DO YOU LOVE DOING?

I've certainly always tried to live my life on the basis that life is precious and to be lived to the full. Many important self-help books have been written on this topic, and my favourites include Viktor Frankl's *Man's Search for Meaning*, which is about finding your own purpose, Bob Buford's *Halftime*, about taking a pause to reflect on the second half of your life, and Martin Hawes's *Twenty Good Summers*, about making the most of your healthy years from age 50 to 70.

This is a different kind of self-help book. It helps people who no longer find their corporate lives to be fulfilling to transition to the NFP sector, where they can do what they like doing, but with a new purpose of doing good.

If you transition without being clear on what you like doing, you may not be happy in your new job. If the first gig you are offered in the NFP sector involves a lot of fundraising but you feel uncomfortable asking for money, then that's not going to work – even if you love the charity's mission.

You might be saying to yourself, 'If I knew what I wanted to do, I'd just do it – but I'm unhappy and I don't know why.' Going back and examining what you really like doing provides a way to get out of that rut.

Make the switch
Sometimes it helps to think back to your childhood and what you spent your time doing. Spending a lot of time making mud pies doesn't mean you want a job making mud pies, of course. It means that you might like to do something that is quite tangible and tactile. You might want to be in the sort of role where you're

helping cook meals or similar. If you love walking in the bush, a role in the environmental area might make you come alive.

Try to reconnect with a time in your life when you were doing what you wanted to do, when you were in flow and weren't even noticing time going by. Career assessment tools can be helpful here, and I discuss these in more detail in chapter 4.

To help you answer this first guiding question about what you love doing, try the following tools for reflection, derived from 'Reawakening your passion for work' by Richard Boyatzis, Annie McKee and Daniel Goleman (from the *Harvard Business Review*). Use the following to hone in on your passion:

*   *Reflect on the past:* Think of the things that you did as a kid that you enjoyed, and that might translate to some aspect of the NFP sector.

*   *Define your principles for life:* Think about the different aspects of your life that are important and what sort of principles in your daily life you might want to try to find satisfaction in when pursuing your NFP career.

*   *Extend the horizon:* What would you like to do with the rest of your life?

*   *Envisage the future:* Imagine you're reading your story 15 years from now and you have lived your ideal life. What sort of fun things would you have done in the NFP sector?

WHAT ARE YOU GOOD AT?

Unless you have something worthwhile to offer in the NFP sector, what's the point of jumping ship? Being aware of your strengths is also important for your own self-confidence along the journey.

I thought that I would have absolutely no relevant skills to take to the NFP sector. The work I was doing in drawing up agreements and advising Australian and international clients on big transactions hardly seemed to fit in with helping kids on the street. You might have similar doubts about whether you have anything worthwhile to offer in a sector that (as I cover in chapter 2) is so different from your corporate world.

You need to focus on the skills that are transferable to the new environment. Sometimes, convincing the people you're working with you do have skills that will be useful to them can take a while.

But you may be surprised. After talking to many coffee buddies and examining my own expertise and experience, I realised that many of my skills would actually be useful in the NFP sector. For example, some of my transferable skills were leading teams, being able to devise and formulate strategy, and providing financial analysis and stakeholder management.

If you're a super-confident person, you might think that the NFP sector will love all your skills. I'm sorry – but that's unlikely to be the case. You need to focus on the skills that are transferable to the new environment. Sometimes, convincing the people you're working with you do have skills that will be useful to them can take a while.

Make the switch

Be careful around those who can't picture your skills being used in any other area. I know many people who are convinced that lawyers are useless apart from their skills in advising clients about legal matters – or maybe that lawyers are just useless. I know that's not the case and I've shown that. As you network with NFP people and learn more about the sector, which of your skills are useful and where in the sector they can be used will become apparent.

To get an idea of your own expectations, do the following exercise: make a list of the principal skills that you have built during your corporate career. Then, in a column next to each skill, write a score out of ten for how useful, if at all, you think that skill might be in the NFP sector. (I look more closely at which of your skills will be transferable in chapter 5.)

In my lawyer years, I used my personality, for want of a better word, to win clients. I wasn't the smartest black letter lawyer in the team, but I was good at winning new deals and building relationships. I didn't think that was relevant for someone who was going to try to help staff support young people in tough environments. But I was a good fundraiser and I could tell people what I was seeing in the streets. After my switch, I had quite a bit of success in bringing in funders and other resources to the organisations I was working with in the NFP sector.

I would have ranked my business development skills as being about four out of ten in term of usefulness – but in fact they turned out to be more like a nine!

WHAT CAUSE ARE YOU PASSIONATE ABOUT?

If you're going to live a satisfying and fulfilling life you love, you'd better make sure that the area you choose in the NFP sector is one you're passionate about. Otherwise, you'll still be working in an unsatisfying job and probably with a lot less pay. The list of NFP causes is long, and includes such diverse areas as guide

> *To find the energy you need to succeed, and the level of commitment to the cause your colleagues and bosses will expect, you'll need to have a strong interest in the cause.*

dogs for the blind or those with low vision, climate change, youth at risk and cancer. You'll likely want some help in finding your NFP needle in the haystack.

To find the energy you need to succeed, and the level of commitment to the cause your colleagues and bosses will expect, you'll need to have a strong interest in the cause. Just as importantly, you'll have a lot more fun if you feel each day that you're working to improve something that's important to you.

You may doubt that it matters exactly which area you start with, as long as you make a difference or give something back. But your colleagues, boss and board will know straightaway if you don't care enough for the cause that is so important to them.

In 'Social return' (published in the *Australian Financial Review's Boss* magazine), the authors interviewed various NFP leaders who used business principles to back social causes. One of them is Michael Traill, the ex-Macquarie banker I mention in chapter 1. The article talks about dealing with approaches from those who don't quite get the NFP sector and are coming from the corporate world. Social researcher Hugh Mackay, who sat on the Social Ventures Australia leadership council, refers to these as 'affluent purpose seekers' and Traill has learned to be wary of them. In the article, Traill talks about how he and colleague Chris Cuffe 'could be up till 4 am every night having coffee with people who want to look you in the eyes and ask, "Have you found it? Why are you doing it? I'm not sure I can keep doing my job for another couple of decades. So what am I going to do with the rest of my life?" '

Traill adds that he has become sceptical about those 'who suddenly declare that it's time "they put something back". They have done no volunteering, have no links with non-profits but reckon they could add a lot of value to a board – any board'.

He steers well clear of 'fix-it-quick' attitudes such as this, for reasons already mentioned in chapter 2 – including greater complexity and the increased number of stakeholders. For Traill, this 'fix-it-quick' approach isn't appropriate, and just won't work.

It is not unreasonable for those working in the NFP sector to be sceptical about business people who suddenly express an interest in the sector, without any track record of past involvement. Identifying a cause that you're passionate about will be important for you in overcoming scepticism like this.

You might be interested in several causes and that's okay. I've always had a strong interest in helping young people facing disadvantage and that's where I've been offered CEO and other leadership roles. But that doesn't mean I don't also feel compassion for, say, older people with mental health issues. Although some leaders do change areas, generally to succeed you must have a deep passion for the cause.

One objective of this book is to provide guidance for those people who are genuine in their search for a new purpose – and who are willing to do the work for a successful switch.

Make the switch

Many of us forget what it's like to be passionate about a cause. Were you angry or an activist as a young person? Back in my university days, I was detained by an officer during the Franklin River protest because I didn't think the nearby Gordon River should be dammed. (This would have flooded the Franklin and destroyed a large wilderness area.)

And although environmental causes concern me, I also feel upset reading about the kind of animal cruelty the RSPCA fights against. But I felt even more angry and upset when Mark Watt shared stories with me about the difficulties that some young people got into out on the street. I felt engaged and that I wanted to be part of that work.

Have you ever just felt your blood boil when you read about something and it makes you say, 'Well, that can't be fair. That's not right. Maybe I could do something about it?'

In chapter 6, I provide more tips on how to find your passion, including what I call the 'newspaper test'. In the meantime, you can begin the process by making a list of all the causes you can think of, and then marking each one's importance to you on a scale of one to ten.

HOW DO YOU LIKE TO WORK?

What form of contribution to a cause suits you? Do you want to work full-time or part-time, and for a large or small organisation?

Just as in the corporate world, finding a role in the NFP sector with the best fit for you will make you happier and more effective. Until I felt a need to change sectors, I was lucky enough to find the perfect fit for me in the corporate world – leading large teams in a preeminent law firm, doing challenging local and international deals. I loved it. Many of my lawyer buddies told me about the joys of their working life in different areas of the law: as a barrister flying solo, mixing personal and professional lives in their close-knit suburban firms, or as an in-house general counsel. But their choice wasn't the best one for me in the legal, corporate world. It's horses for courses and it's the same in the NFP world.

As I got to know more people in the NFP sector and asked them for their thoughts on what might be the best fit for me, given my corporate experience at the big end of town, most of them thought I'd end up as a senior executive at one of the large international NGOs. However, my CEO and 2IC roles have been with small to mid-sized NFPs. This was a surprise to me, but it just seemed a better fit, at least in the initial stages of my switching journey.

Most of the NFP people I've met have found a particular fit in the sector. It's like their personal brand. For me, the fit has been with organisations serving young people and their families facing disadvantage, across various roles – such as CEO, COO, 2IC, as a member of the executive team, being on the service-delivery side or being on the philanthropic side. I've experimented with all those things and the best fit I've found to date is as a CEO in a medium-sized organisation providing services to people facing disadvantage. But who knows what the future holds?

Make the switch

Here's an exercise to start you thinking about how and where you might like to work. Write down all the characteristics of your current working mode. Pick the factors that seem most important to you at this stage of the process. Is this more flexibility? Working full-time? Less interstate travel? Working in the CBD? Travelling under ten kilometres to work? Working from home? Working in Australia? Working in an open plan office? Having a more understanding boss? Working with small teams or larger hierarchy? In a small or large organisation? No more time sheets? Having less stress? Being a CEO, senior executive or team member? Being part of the front line? Once you've finished your list, rate each item with a score out of ten (with ten being your ideal condition).

GETTING HELP FROM A CAREER COACH

The four guiding questions I've outlined in this chapter can be difficult to grapple with on your own. And having someone beside you when you hit bumps along your switching journey is worthwhile – as is having someone to gently nudge you when you are struggling to do the necessary networking.

An internet search will provide a long list of career coaches in your city. If you decide to consider a career coach, make sure you feel the right connection – you want someone with whom you can share your innermost thoughts. And you want someone who challenges you and provides helpful insights about yourself – especially if you come from a background where your employer didn't invest in helping you understand yourself. Experience with switching to the NFP sector would be advantageous, but is not common and not essential. A recommendation from someone you trust is a good start.

WRAP UP

You now have an overview of the four-question framework I used to transition to the NFP sector. These are the four essential questions that guided my journey and can guide yours too.

You can do the exercises set out in this chapter to get a feel for your current state of mind – and then read the following chapters to take you into the future.

You may have 'quite liked' the sort of work you have been doing in the past. Now is your chance to do work that you *love* doing, maybe for the first time in your working life. Doesn't that sound exciting? The next chapter explores how.

FOUR

What do you love doing?

I love helping young people to live the best lives they can – whether it's my own children, junior staff members or young people whom I mentor. But it wasn't until after I had switched sectors that doing something I love became the purpose of my everyday working life.

I also love bushwalking – and had to pinch myself when my work in the not-for-profit (NFP) sector saw me getting paid while I was out bushwalking with young colleagues and clients.

What you love doing, in the context of your not-for-profit role, is extremely personal. In chapter 1, I cover finding meaning in your life by transitioning to an NFP role. In the previous chapter, I briefly outlined the four guiding questions to guide that transition. This chapter deals with the first of those questions in more depth: finding the things you love doing in your day-to-day work. Having a job with meaning is pointless if there's no fun in it. And, as the saying goes, 'Choose a job you love, and you will never have to work a day in your life.'

In chapter 1, I discussed thinking about what you want to get out of your life. There aren't many bigger questions than contemplating how you want to best use your time on this planet. Breaking that big question into smaller pieces helps, starting with a question such as: 'How do I want to spend my time?' This is an easier question than 'What should I do?', but will probably lead to the same answer.

If you don't like many things about your current work, such as filling out boring monthly reports for your manager, now is the time to find a role where you like most things.

When you have spare time, what do you like doing? Do you prefer being creative, working with numbers, spending time outdoors, ticking off admin tasks or helping people? The list of possibilities is endless, but the answer will be specific to you as an individual.

You might like spending more time with people than your current role allows, so you can find a role in the NFP sector that has more people contact. This is a great opportunity to reinvent a job and put in the bits that you like, because if you've spent a reasonable amount of time working in the corporate sector, you will have a pretty good idea of what you do and don't like.

I'm basing my advice on my own experience and what successful NFP leaders have told me. Although I loved being a mergers and acquisitions lawyer, in the later years I found that I was enjoying it less – particularly when it meant working through the weekends, long hours, tight deadlines and continual emails and phone calls from demanding clients. But I still enjoyed bringing in new deals, which is a form of networking. I loved running the teams when the work came in, organising, and getting the best results for a common cause. But, frankly, I was over the hours and the grind. By going through the process of analysing my preferences, I found a new working life filled with things I love doing.

To help clarify what you like doing in a work context, take these three steps:

1. Use a career assessment tool.

2. Talk to people who know you.

3. Do your own sense check.

USE A CAREER ASSESSMENT TOOL

By a career assessment tool, I mean psychological and career aptitude testing. Several options are available, including the (largely discredited) Myers-Briggs Type Indicator, but one that I used is the Birkman Method, which measures behaviours, needs and interests. If you decide to consider retaining a career coach, this early stage of assessment is a good time to do it.

These tools can provide an objective measure of your areas of interest; for example, clerical, scientific, numerical, outdoor or mechanical.

I recommend the Birkman Method. After taking the test, you're given a nice thick folder with lots of graphs, which I went through with my career coach, who was trained to do the analysis. You can use the test to start thinking about the sorts of places where the things that you like to do actually happen. After taking the test, it became clear to me that I didn't want to stay any longer in the corporate world, even if I changed to doing more good in that world. I read the results of my test and it was like an epiphany.

Whatever tool you use, you will want to talk through the results with someone. If it's an online test, maybe talk with a friend or colleague. If the test is administered professionally, talk to the person who administers it – in my case, my career coach – and explore where jobs might emerge in the areas of interest that you really like.

As I mentioned in chapter 1, I did a test using the Birkman Method in 2009, when I was starting to think about what I might do after my career in the law. I did the test again in 2014, by which time I was ready to transition and look for a role in the NFP sector. Comparing my results for the two Birkman tests showed a significant drop in the 'clerical' area of interest, but ongoing interest and high scores in 'social work' and 'teaching'. The career coach who conducted the test said, 'If you were leaving high school, Steve, I would be telling you that you should be a social worker or a teacher. Law is there, but it's low.' Although I had loved being a lawyer for several decades, my interests had changed dramatically.

This began a reflective process for me that reminded me of things I liked. It also brought to my attention some things I used to like but no longer liked as much. The spike in the outdoor area of interest was intriguing – particularly for someone who's spent his whole life sitting inside an office with clients. My career coach said, 'What's this all about?' I told him that one of my absolute passions in life has always been hiking, and it was way more than a hobby. That's what I love doing in my spare time. Interestingly, after having spent the last eight years working in the NFP sector, most of the organisations I've worked with have programs that get young people outside to help them reconnect with the important things in life.

Make the switch

Find a career assessment tool that you think is worthwhile and take it. Several are available online.

TALK TO PEOPLE WHO KNOW YOU

Using a career assessment tool is a good start, but the next step is talking to people you know. You need a sounding board to help you identify your areas of interest. I found it very helpful talking about my likes and dislikes with my wife, friends, mentors and trusted colleagues. They'll call your bluff. For example, if I'd said my passion was food, they might have said, 'Steve, you don't actually like brussels sprouts. You just wish that you did because you think they're good for you.' Let's say I'd said I wanted to go to Africa and ensure poverty or hunger didn't exist anywhere in the world. 'Well, really, let's be practical about this, Steve. You wouldn't actually want to live outside Australia.'

> *You need a sounding board to help you identify your areas of interest. I found it very helpful talking about my likes and dislikes with my wife, friends, mentors and trusted colleagues. They'll call your bluff.*

You might doubt that you can find any sort of NFP work that matches your areas of likes. And you might be right (but I doubt it). But let's at least ask the question. If you don't find anything, then so be it, but you don't want to die wondering. In my case, it turned out that I could find roles that involved elements of social work, teaching and even the outdoors. And just a little bit of the other stuff such as clerical and admin skills.

Make the switch

Talk with your partner, friends, mentors and trusted colleagues. Do you know anyone with a connection to the NFP sector? Ask them to assist with clarifying your thoughts over a coffee, starting with the ones you know well. One of the people I talked to said, 'Look, you really should have a career coach, and here's who I used.' So I explored whether a career coach might help me – and decided to get one.

If you have used a career assessment tool, talk your results through with one of your family members, friends or colleagues. Ask them, 'Do these findings make sense to you? Are they the "me" you know?'

This allows you to road test the results of this objective test with someone who knows you well. You're taking out your internal reflections and testing them with trusted friends and colleagues. Take your top three scores and ask them, 'Which of these three do you think is on the top, from your knowledge of me?'

If you have a partner, their thoughts will be vital. This early stage is also a good time to discuss with them their thoughts about switching sectors. Apart from the likely financial implications, the transition process involves a lot of time and effort. If your partner is not supportive of your move to the NFP sector, you'd better find out sooner rather than later. You may need to bring them along with you on your journey. Switching without partner support would be a challenge, to say the least.

DO YOUR OWN SENSE CHECK

Query yourself about your findings from any career assessment tools or chats with those closest to you. Do these results seem right? If, for example, you've never been in a tent in your life and the assessment tool says you like the outdoors, it wouldn't seem right. When I discussed the results of my Birkman test with my career coach, it was an epiphany and absolute confirmation of what I'd been feeling but hadn't been able to enunciate. For others, the sense checking might be a slow dawn or a finessing of ideas that they already had. Take all the information you've received from the test, your career coach and your friends, and go into another process of reflection. Is this who you really are? Are you starting to discover from those discussions what you love doing?

My sense checking confirmed the Birkman results, and what I was hearing from people who knew me. In the corporate world I had loved mentoring and teaching members of my teams, helping them to bring out their best. I enjoyed the social work aspects of helping people facing disadvantage in my volunteering outside work. Even the outdoors piece fell into place, as I came to lead organisations that ran outdoor programs.

Although people you know may have a good idea of what you're like at work, they may be biased with limitations that it's time to remove. They may have difficulty seeing you doing anything other than what they have seen you doing in the past. But now you've used a career assessment tool, you've talked about it with your close friends and colleagues, and you've done a sense check yourself. Put all that together and you've got an authentic answer to the question, 'What do I love doing?' that you can start plugging into potential roles.

Imagine the joy you will feel when you find that job where you do what you love doing!

I still remember the satisfaction of my first role – as chief operating officer at Whitelion, working with youth at risk. How right it felt to be working in a role where I was actually doing what I liked doing – working to bring out the best in a team who mentored, taught, and provided social work and outdoor programs. Imagine the joy you will feel when you find that job where you do what you love doing!

Make the switch

When you reach the sense check stage, you're trying to put together the results of the career assessment tool, the comments of your friends and colleagues, and your own overlay of what seems right to you. At this stage, I've found it useful to ask myself, 'Do I really like doing these things? Would I do them for nothing, without being paid a cent?'

As an exercise, make a list of all the things that you love doing. To finesse the process, rate how much you enjoy each item on your list with a score out of ten (with ten being the thing you most love doing).

WRAP UP

This chapter aims to help you understand what you love doing at work. I hope you'll now proceed to use a career assessment tool (and perhaps a career coach), talk to friends and colleagues, and then complete a sense check on yourself.

But what skills can you offer your new sector? That's the question I explore in the next chapter.

FIVE

What are you good at?

A senior corporate lawyer decides to switch sectors after many years to lead a youth charity. How on Earth did his first career provide any skills relevant for his second?

We all have some skills and expertise that are transferable to the not-for-profit (NFP) sector, and a successful transition requires you to know what skills you have to offer. A transferable skill is a skill that was useful for you in the corporate world, that you can now use in a completely different context. For example, networking in the corporate world might translate into bringing in business and earning revenue, whereas networking in the NFP sector might mean bringing in funds and resources to an under-resourced organisation or using your connections to collaborate with another NFP. It's the same skill, but used in a different way.

Why would you want to take on an NFP role that you don't have the skills for? If you're going to convince your first employer to hire you, you're going to need a good pitch about how the skills you've been using and developing during your time in the corporate world will be useful and relevant in this new context. I strongly believe additional skills are needed in this resource-strapped sector and I would like to see more corporate transitions helping to meet that need.

Being aware of your transferable skills will give you the confidence to push ahead with this transition, help you find a role that uses those skills, and help you convince that first employer to take you on. I feel fortunate that I was headhunted for each of the roles I have had in the sector. But I believe this occurred because I was always very clear with people about what skills I had to offer (and what my weaknesses were). I also rewrote my CV and LinkedIn profile to highlight those of my skills that would be more attractive in the NFP world – having 'extensive senior business networks' may or may not be useful in business, but sends a strong message to NFP boards that you are likely to be the kind of CEO who is comfortable getting out and about and pitching for funding and other resources. I dropped aspects that were simply related to law from my CV and LinkedIn profile – even though I might have been very proud of them – because they were no longer of use in my new sector.

Being aware of your transferable skills will give you the confidence to push ahead with this transition, help you find a role that uses those skills, and help you convince that first employer to take you on.

In the first section of this chapter, I outline about how to (bravely!) ask your corporate colleagues about your skills and expertise, especially in the way that you work. Next, I look at which of your skills and experience may be transferable to the NFP sector. Finally, I discuss how to identify any gaps in your skills.

ASK WHAT OTHERS THINK

Be brave and ask your corporate colleagues about your skills and expertise, especially in the way that they have seen you work. Kidding yourself that you have skills that you don't have is pointless, as is not realising how your skills could translate into the NFP sector. Although it can be confronting, I found that approaching people who knew my corporate style well could provide helpful insights. Also important is asking people who know you well about your weaknesses – this can makes you feel vulnerable, but the self-awareness that emerges is really valuable. Through this chapter, I suggest some questions to ask.

With the guidance of my career coach, Bill Cowan, I sent a confidential email to about half a dozen long-standing clients and close business colleagues. I told them I was working with a coach to examine various career options and asked for them to identify my 'special strengths'. Specifically, the email asked them to spend a few minutes to provide some honest dot points under four headings:

1. the way I think

2. the way I work with people (particularly teams)

3. the way I communicate

4. any other strengths not already included.

Note that these headings focus only on strengths at this stage, not weaknesses. My questioning process resulted in answers that I would never have thought of myself. I'd expected references to my being 'energetic' and 'a people person', but several responses also referred to me as someone who 'thinks outside the square'.

Based on the surprisingly consistent responses, I rewrote my CV to include the following strengths: thinking outside the square, bringing out the best in people, having energy and tenacity to get things done, being an articulate and engaging communicator, and staying cool in a crisis. False modesty has no purpose in this process – I expect that you'll be pleasantly surprised by some of the feedback you receive!

You may doubt the wisdom of asking for insights in these areas from business colleagues when you're not sure that a transition out of the corporate world is what you really want. What if you ask your best client about these personal issues? Will they doubt your future commitment if you decide not to proceed with the transition? It requires some bravery, but you can always retrace your steps and tell your client you decided to stay on in your existing field of work.

In my case, I sent these emails at a time when I was not 100 per cent committed to switching, but pretty sure that this was what I wanted to do. If I had changed my mind, I could have gone back to those clients and explained that I had decided to stay on as a lawyer.

Sending the confidential email to my clients actually showed the great trust I had in them, which they respected. I said, 'This is confidential because I haven't told my CEO yet that I'm thinking of a new career.' These clients could have taken my questions as a lack of commitment to the law and to their interests, distanced themselves, and moved on to find another lawyer. But it actually strengthened my relationships with them. If I had decided to come back to the law, I'm sure those relationships would have been better for having gone through this process. In each case, they were interested in my journey and continue to keep in touch to this day. In several cases, they ended up supporting the NFPs I later joined as a leader.

Make the switch

Make a list of six to ten people who know you well in a corporate context. Ask them for feedback in the four areas I've outlined in this section. Remind them they need to be frank and honest in their answers.

If you've started your research while still working in your corporate job and haven't yet mentioned your idea to your boss or colleagues, make sure your respondents are trustworthy and understand the importance of confidentiality.

TRANSFERABLE SKILLS

Some people struggle to see any of their skills from the corporate world as being relevant in the NFP context. Indeed, people who are subject matter experts tend to forget that they have transferable skills at all. They are too focused on their specific expertise, and their skills that are unlikely to have direct application in the NFP world – for example, if they are a mineral geologist.

However, dig a little deeper, and many examples of possible transferable skills can be found, including those gained from:

- leading teams

- strategic planning

- financial acumen

- stakeholder management.

These are all good examples of skills that many corporates have and that can be used in another context. If seeing your transferable skills is presenting a barrier for you, consider your experience in these other areas and the skills you have gained from them. Of course you may have skills that do have direct application in the NFP world (for example, in HR, finance or IT). If so, you are lucky – and so is the charity that snaps you up!

> *Identifying your transferable skills is important because NFPs are resource-strapped. To get that first gig, you need to show them you're bringing as many relevant and useful skills as you can.*

Identifying your transferable skills is important because NFPs are resource-strapped. To get that first gig, you need to show them you're bringing as many relevant and useful skills as you can.

When I was at the skilled volunteering stage of my transition (covered in chapter 9), I started joining Whitelion's monthly senior executive meetings as an observer, providing comments on areas as diverse as strategy, HR and staff matters, financials and fundraising. When the chief operating officer resigned a couple of months later, I was offered his role because it was clear to the CEO and board that with one hire and one salary they could cover off on all of those areas.

You may not think your corporate background brings any skills that will be useful in the NFP sector. Initially, I asked myself what skills a senior mergers and acquisitions lawyer would be able to bring to a charity providing services for at-risk youth facing disadvantage. But by going through this process, I realised I'd underestimated the transferable skills I did have. I'm sure you will discover from this process, as I did, that you have transferable skills you didn't even realise you have.

Make the switch

Begin by undertaking an honest review of your work skills. Consider the following areas, and your experience and skills in these, to assist your review:

- leading teams
- finding simple solutions to complex problems
- risk management
- financial acumen
- good business networks (for example, for fundraising, partnerships)
- articulate communication and advocating
- strategic planning
- governance
- specific subject matter areas, such as HR, IT, legal and regulatory.

Give yourself a score out of ten as to how proficient you think you are at each skill you have listed.

You may struggle to do this on your own and to be sufficiently objective. As I was initially, you may be too hard on yourself and not see any transferable skills. Feel free to enlist the help of one or more colleagues to ensure that you don't omit anything.

Through the course of this book, I advise relying a great deal on your friends, family and colleagues. It's important that they're part of this journey.

The answers in response to the special strengths email you can send to your old work colleagues (refer to the section 'Ask what others think', earlier in this chapter) may also provide some ideas here. Your coffee buddies and networking options should also help in writing your skills list. (See chapter 8 for more on networking, and maintaining a spreadsheet that includes insights gained from these contacts.) Someone you're having coffee with may give you a couple of ideas of skill areas that you hadn't thought of. In your next coffee meeting, if the other person can't think of any transferable skills, you can help by saying, 'Well, what about A, B, C?' parroting back the ideas you'd been told before. They then might provide a view on those ideas – or ideally suggest some more. In this way, you're constantly building knowledge. And the more experience you have asking for this feedback, the better you become at receiving and giving it. The difference was stark for me between coffee number one, when I was standing there saying, 'What the hell am I doing?', compared to coffee 171, when I felt that I had much more value to add to the discussion.

GAPS IN SKILLS

Up to now, I've taken a strengths-based approach on where your transferable skills lie. I've advised building on things you're good at, rather than trying to improve areas where you're weak. The concept of strength-based actions seems at odds with the dog-eat-dog culture of the corporate world, but you'll likely come across it everywhere in the NFP sector.

But what are your weaknesses in the NFP context?

If you're going to be the irresistible addition to that NFP team you would love to join, covering off any major gaps in your skills is also important. This could involve studying a relevant course. It will likely involve internet research and reading to better understand the Australian NFP sector and the issues relevant to its numerous stakeholders. And no doubt you'll make use of a lot of Q&A while networking.

Initially I had thought the NFP sector can't be that different, and I'd be able to build up the skills and required sector knowledge as I went along. But, as discussed in chapter 2, the sectors are very different and my learning curve was huge.

I was entering the NFP sector at a senior executive level after 30 years in the corporate sector. I had been involved in advising and supporting charities in the NFP sector even when I'd been in corporate, so I had that background to build on. I was then able to gain a huge amount of information on the job about the sector, the programs run by my NFP, and about funding by government and other sources. I didn't end up going back to university to get a relevant degree or a diploma, although I had considered doing that. If I'd made the switch earlier, such as in my twenties or thirties, I would certainly have completed a course – for example, a master's in social work or a master's in international development. (As a sidenote, Deakin University in Victoria has a master's in humanitarian assistance, developed with Save the Children, and it sounds fascinating.) In addition to universities, online learning is also available, along with specific NFP courses run by organisations such as People for Purpose or the Australian Institute of Company Directors.

> *If you're going to be the irresistible addition to that NFP team you would love to join, covering off any major gaps in your skills is also important.*

I considered these options, but – as I was lucky enough to have gained roles in the sector – decided to continue my training on the job. As I said, the learning curve was huge, and this did lead to some bumpy days.

MY WORST DAY

Tuesday 25 October 2016 was a day I will never forget. It was the day when I felt my skills were so lacking that maybe switching had been a big mistake.

Here's what happened.

I had been appointed by Save the Children on a six-month contract as head of Australian operations, to lead a team of experienced state managers with much greater knowledge of the programs than I would ever have. I was keen to make a difference as quickly as possible and started giving advice soon after my arrival. Some of them felt that I hadn't taken the time to learn about their programs or their approach before I started making suggestions to improve them. And they weren't happy about it.

I could tell that things weren't going as well as I had hoped, so I discussed with HR what action we might take. They suggested a 'new manager assimilation' (NMA) exercise, which I had never heard of – but now will never forget!

An NMA is an HR-facilitated discussion designed to accelerate the 'getting to know you process' between a new leader and their direct reports, specifically focusing on mutual understanding, communication and operating styles. It sounded like a good idea – and I willingly accepted their offer to organise an NMA for me and the team. I wanted to be the best I could be – and to add maximum value during my time at Save the Children.

My NMA took place during the national offsite held each year for the senior leadership group. I had arranged with my old law firm to provide a venue in their offices (at no charge, of course).

The HR team asked me to leave the meeting room during the initial discussion, to encourage frank and honest feedback. When I eventually returned to the room, seeing walls covered with butcher's paper emblazoned with bold red marker pen scribbles, it was clear that the discussion had been frank and forthright!

As the HR team started the debrief, I noticed that several people looked a bit uncomfortable. At first, I couldn't work out why.

We started with the positive feedback from the state managers – they were aware of my previous corporate work and that I had a family. They knew I was motivated with strong values, energy and drive. I was friendly and took an interest in people, and I was open to feedback to change my behaviour and impact if required. A reasonable start to the debrief.

But they were also very clear that this ex-corporate had plenty of room for improvement! In particular, the large red notes on the butcher's paper highlighted the following:

- I was trying to build relationships too quickly.

- I had a lawyerly approach.

- I was too quick to form strong opinions.

- I didn't always understand the context of a situation.

- I asked a lot of questions but not the right ones.

- I focused on the wrong things.

Overall, the feedback was along the lines of, 'He's a nice guy but he doesn't listen enough. He doesn't understand our programs. He's too pushy. He wants to move too fast to make things better, but we're not even sure what's wrong. He asks the wrong questions about how to improve, to grow, to be more efficient before he properly understands what our actual programs are.'

The exercise showed the differences between how the state managers approached what they were doing as experts and how I came in as a corporate, with different expertise but trying to make things more efficient and effective, in a hurry.

The NFP sector is a so-called soft sector – and a large law firm is a notoriously tough environment. In fact, over the years I had given and received some pretty tough feedback in those very corporate offices where the NMA was held. But I doubt that those offices have seen many experiences as confronting as my NMA session that afternoon!

I was devastated.

I went home thinking, *Do I really want to play this game? Do I really want to start a new career? Maybe I can just go back to my previous career, keep doing a really good job as a lawyer but focus more on legal work for the NFP sector. That's good enough, isn't it?*

I suppose some people might have given up at that stage. But, deep down, I knew what I wanted to do with my life. I wanted to keep going, learn more and build on what I had already achieved. I had asked people to be tough on me and to give me strong feedback – and now they had done so, I needed to take this feedback on board.

Later that night, after dinner, I received text messages from some of the senior people who had been in that room, checking that I was alright. They all basically said the same thing: 'We were tough on you. You did ask us to not hold back and to be upfront, and we did what you asked. But you impressed everyone with your humble response, and your willingness to act on the feedback, so don't give up.'

When I was interstate soon after the NMA, one state manager sat me down and gave me some advice about listening – for example, how to sit facing someone, and how to 'mirror' them (that is, mimic postures and gestures to show empathy and build rapport). I was surprised to hear that this kind of soft skill was so important for an NFP leader. In the business world, you're not likely to be taught the art of mirroring. But my manager was doing me a favour. Maybe I was a good listener by corporate standards, but I still had a long way to go in the NFP world.

The NMA was a great learning experience for me, starkly highlighting a gap in my skills, knowledge and approach. From that day on, in every organisation where I have had a leadership role, I've made sure that I meet as many staff as possible in the early days, and get a good working knowledge as soon as possible of the programs run by the organisation. At the end of the day, when you're leading a team that is mainly about service delivery, what those people in your team live and breathe is their program. They want you to ask questions about it. They're not bored by these questions and they don't feel you're wasting their time – this is their life.

Nowadays my first step when meeting new staff is to listen, ask questions and then listen some more. Curiosity and humility are key ingredients to success here.

Know your weaknesses. It's the old story – if you've stuffed up something really badly, the lessons in life you gain from the stuff-up are the ones you never forget. I have no doubt that the lessons learnt have made me a better leader. They were largely responsible for my subsequent two years as CEO of Doxa being so successful for that organisation and its leadership team.

My first step when meeting new staff is to listen, ask questions and then listen some more. Curiosity and humility are key ingredients to success here.

Although I still carry the scars, I am so grateful for what I learnt from my colleagues on that October day.

Make the switch

Review what gaps may exist in the skills you are bringing to the NFP sector. The best way to do this is to ask your colleagues and your networking contacts about any weaknesses you need to address, and collate their answers. (As covered in chapter 8, addressing your weaknesses is one of the three key areas to discuss during your networking meetings.) Do any themes emerge? What suggestions do your colleagues or networking buddies have on how to deal with those gaps? Do they suggest any courses, or reading or research that would help to fill the gap?

As a human being, asking about where you have weaknesses can be confronting and uncomfortable. You need to be brave and make sure you involve some colleagues. Presumably you've come from a career in the corporate world where you've had some success and now you're being told that you don't know what you're talking about in this new sector. Colleagues can provide perspective on this. You might have to go back to learning again, do a course, and maybe find yourself sitting next to much younger people at university. This could appear daunting.

But try turning that viewpoint around. I would say this is a wonderful opportunity you now have at this stage of your life, where you've ticked off a corporate career and built some wonderful skills there. And you can take those skills and build on them to make a difference in the NFP sector. You can learn again and get excited about taking on new challenges and new skills. To me, that's not something you should be upset about – it's a gift.

WRAP UP

You now know how to identify your transferable skills – not just what you do, but also how you do it – and if you have any gaps that you need to address. You need to be brave and involve colleagues to help with this review of your skills. Reach out and ask for feedback. Do the work to identify what transferable skills you have and then test drive that list on your NFP network. You'll find that some skills are more useful than you think.

But having wonderful, transferable skills to offer the sector is pointless if you don't know what cause you are passionate about. In the next chapter, I help you find out what lights your fire.

SIX

What cause are you passionate about?

The cause you're passionate about may have appeared in the newspaper you read yesterday. Or it may have inspired the chocolate brownies you made years ago for your high school fundraiser.

This chapter is about identifying the cause that makes you upset or angry, because that will provide helpful energy for a successful transition. You may be passionate about more than one cause, though it helps to focus on just one to start with.

Myriad good causes are represented by worthwhile community organisations – including education, housing, environment, employment, young people, health, domestic violence, substance abuse, sport and recreation, arts, justice, animals, medical research, crisis support and community organisations. The list goes on and on.

If you can identify which cause means a lot to you as a person, you'll find more satisfaction in the NFP sector, and the enthusiasm coming from that will mean you're more likely to succeed. If you don't identify with your cause, you might just find yourself filling in time doing good but not doing your best work.

Early on, I was tempted to take on a couple of great leadership roles simply because they were offered to me – a CEO role in the medical research area and one in a creative arts organisation. Although I was keen to find a role in the NFP sector, in the end I declined both offers, with some trepidation, because I wasn't passionate about their cause. I knew I wouldn't have brought the necessary drive to inspire myself and my team.

In this chapter, I start with what I call the 'newspaper test', along with looking at alternative methods for uncovering what really fires you up. Next, I discuss how to test-drive your cause. Finally, I ask you to consider whether there could be a perfect cause you didn't even know about. By following these three steps, you can identify which cause or causes are important to you. Rather than just relying on your own thoughts, you can double-check with people who know you well. You can also do some research to make sure you've considered as many causes as possible.

If you can identify which cause means a lot to you as a person, you'll find more satisfaction in the NFP sector

THE NEWSPAPER TEST

When you open a newspaper, whether it's an online or paper version, what articles fire you up? What makes you upset or angry? These reactions provide guidance in a very simple overall way, without spending hours researching every NFP and cause under the sun.

I used to say that I studied law because I wanted to change the world. It seemed to me that advocating for social justice was one reason many of us lawyers started studying law. But it didn't take long for more materialistic motivations to appear, especially when I was faced with the costs of raising a family. The question as to how I could best contribute to society was postponed for a while.

Over the years I often reflected on how poverty seemed to be the biggest and toughest problem on the planet. Wouldn't it be great to spend my last working years devoted to ending global poverty? That idea didn't seem inconsistent with my idealistic thoughts back when I started studying law. As I started to think more about switching to make a greater contribution to society, one of my mentors suggested that the newspaper test might help me.

When I did the newspaper test and reflected on what made me angry and upset, I asked myself about the cause that resonated with me. I realised that stories about young people in Australia, supposedly the lucky country, who were facing such unfair challenges and disadvantage in their lives, were the ones that made me the most upset. These were stories about poverty, hunger, domestic abuse, homelessness and youth justice. It didn't seem fair. From an early age, these young people didn't have the same opportunities that had been available to me and my family and friends. I could find no justice in my three children having led such a fortunate life, when so many other Aussie kids had not.

After I had worked through the newspaper test, I eventually found a role working for the right cause for me. I knew what kinds of inequities upset me so that, when I was having a hard day at work, I could say to myself, 'At least I am trying to make a difference in some small way, so that when I open the paper in the future, there won't be as many stories about that particular issue.'

One of the things I struggled with was focusing on just one particular cause after doing the newspaper test – what about all the other people and the other causes that I'm leaving behind? Environmental issues such as global warming worry me a lot, but I realised I'm happy to leave those causes to other people who are more passionate than me. One friend did attack my philosophy by saying, 'Look, Steve, wasting your time helping troubled kids is pointless. If you don't come and support our climate change cause, there won't even be a planet for those kids to live on.' That may or may not be true. But I decided that I would just have to leave others to tackle those other causes that still upset me. You'll have a lot more impact if you focus on the cause that you're most passionate about.

If you read the newspaper and found nothing specifically that troubles you with the state of the world, you might wonder whether you do want to work in this sector. Maybe you want to do something else with your energies in this stage of your life. Maybe you want to work in a hospital or university. Or you'd like to improve things generally in the world, but nothing specific. That's fine, because you can offer your services and someone will snap up your general desire to do some good. Or maybe you need to read more widely – newspapers from different publishers, along with global magazines. Or maybe your cause isn't in the news at the moment. The newspaper test is quite simplistic and doesn't always work. Don't worry if that's the case; I discuss some alternative strategies in the next section.

Make the switch

Do the newspaper test on yourself. Read newspaper articles for a couple of days in a row, and see what fires you up. Think about the stories that have troubled you when listening to the news, reading the paper or watching the TV, both in the past and the present.

OTHER OPTIONS FOR FINDING YOUR CAUSE

If you are still working in the corporate sector, you have a great opportunity to examine your social conscience using your past behaviour. What areas have you supported as a donor or volunteer in your past private and corporate lives? In my corporate life, I had great exposure to a lot of charities as chairman of the charity committee at our law firm. That also helped to fine-tune the causes I was interested in.

One year, the charity committee received an application requesting money for a wheelchair for a young person who was suffering from a debilitating physical disease. The younger lawyers were keen to approve a grant but I remember thinking, *It's a really sad story, but at least that kid's got a loving family. What about all the young people out there who are sleeping rough or in the detention centres?*

I had the chance to look at lots of applications from other good causes and fine-tune my own ideas. But different people will have different causes they're passionate about. This is your chance to find out what yours is.

Every now and then over recent years, I have had moments of clarity where I feel the significance to me personally of working to change young lives. For example, Doxa Youth Foundation, where I worked as CEO, runs 'journey programs' where teenagers from disadvantaged backgrounds go on overnight or multi-day bushwalks with trained outdoor educators. The experience of being out in the bush, away from the challenges of their everyday lives, working as a team with the other campers, can literally be life-changing.

As we hiked along on one journey program, I overheard a young person (let's call him Sam) talking about his future job options with one of the leaders, who was a trained youth worker. Sam eventually shared he had once wanted to be a paramedic but had dropped the idea 'because my mum reckons I'm too dumb to do the course'. To cut a long story short, during that three-day hike the leader had several conversations with Sam about his abilities and his future options. By the time he returned to the bus, Sam was determined to pursue the possibility of becoming a paramedic – with the leader as his committed mentor going forward. Witnessing Sam's transformation gave me an intense feeling that, although the corporate world had been great, this was the right place for me at this stage of my life.

While you're in the corporate sector, perhaps you can get involved with your organisation's charity committee or some aspect of its environmental, social and governance (ESG) work. This might allow you to see similar transformations closer up, and con-

> 'The change you are seeking may be closer than you think.'

sider how they solidify your passion for a particular cause. One of my mentors said to me, 'The change you are seeking may be closer than you think.' I remember wondering what they were telling me with those strange words, which sounded like something straight out of a kung fu TV series. But I now realise how common it is to find yourself involved with NFPs that you knew from your corporate days.

After getting involved with your organisation's charity committee (or similar), you may want to then take your volunteering to a deeper level with a cause that interests you, by exploring the possibility of serving on an NFP board. This can also be a potential route to a management position, although I am not aware of many successful board-to-CEO transfers. Despite being offered board roles from time to time, I was keen to put all my time and energy into a leadership role, and I told my mentors accordingly. I expect that down the track an NFP board role may be of interest to me.

Another aspect to consider is what you like doing in your non-work life. If animals are a big part of your non-working life, for example, maybe an organisation such as the RSPCA is for you. Looking back, I realised I'd occasionally thought about volunteering at one of the charities that takes young people into the bush to help them break the cycle of their daily challenges, but I never did. My Birkman Method test score had a very high ranking on the outdoors. Three of the causes I ended up working with had outdoor programs. My mentor was right – what you're looking for may be closer than you think.

As well as helping you find your passion, past involvement with causes can help build credibility when you're talking to a potential employer or to future work colleagues. Earlier in this book I mentioned the common focus in the NFP sector on 'we don't care what you know, until we know you care'. Being able to say I'd been mentoring young people at Doxa and been a fundraiser for the Whitelion Bailout for many years gave me validity when I was looking at employment with those organisations years later.

Similarly, when I was asked to take on the CEO role at SecondBite, it helped to be able to say I had been a corporate supporter back in my 'suit and tie' days. I had even been a volunteer on one of their food collection vans.

Make the switch

If the newspaper test doesn't work for you, or you want to get some further insights into what your area or cause might be, try one of the following methods:

- Have you made donations to any charities over the years? Which ones?

- Which TV news item or coverage on one of the public affairs shows often fires you up?

- What about the movies? Do the ones about kids dying of cancer particularly move you?

- Which charity would you consider giving up your precious time to support as a volunteer without getting paid?

While you're waiting for your first NFP gig, look to volunteer in an area of passion. In chapter 9, I talk about how you can use volunteering to get your first employed gig. But, in the meantime, volunteering is a way to test which areas evoke your passion, along with providing that future credibility.

You might find it difficult to clarify your thoughts about what makes you angry or upset. If that's the case, try addressing that barrier using one of the alternative methods from this section. And just give the process some time. You may not have thought about these deep issues for a long time, so don't be too impatient. I spoke to several mentors to finesse and test-drive my passion for different causes. Michael Traill's advice to me was not to worry if I couldn't readily identify a passion, because something would come along that was just right. This was excellent advice, even though in my case it didn't take me very long to find a passion in tackling youth disadvantage.

TEST-DRIVE YOUR CAUSE

Once you've decided on the cause that you think is most important to you, ask people around you for their thoughts. Your partner, your family, your friends, your business colleagues, your mentors, the network that you're building up over your coffee chats – all of them will be able to give you some input. Do they agree this is the right passion for you to pursue? Do they have any other thoughts?

These people provide a good filter and by test-driving your thinking this way, as it develops, you'll minimise the risk of picking the wrong cause and you'll fine-tune as you go along.

Early on, I was worried about whether or not I would find a job in the sector because role models of people who had successfully switched were hard to find. When I was offered an NFP CEO role quite early in the process, I was flattered and relieved.

I said to my wife, 'Good news. I've been offered a gig. But I don't know if I should take it or not.'

She said, 'Hang on. You've never been interested in that area before.' It was great to have her input, knowing my personality as she does, and I ultimately declined the offer.

Even if your family or friends don't know enough about the NFP sector to suggest which cause within it will be right for you, they do know you. If they say, 'You've always had a soft spot for helping old people,' and you agree with them, maybe you should look into working with the NFP aged care organisations.

Even if your family or friends don't know enough about the NFP sector to suggest which cause within it will be right for you, they do know you.

It's okay if you can't find just one cause. Test-driving two or three may help to narrow your options down to your preferred sector, or prioritise them in a certain order. One example of that comes from when I was thinking about working with an overseas NFP – see chapter 7 for more detail on this decision, and my reasoning as I made it.

Make the switch

Once you have an idea of the cause you'd like to pursue, ask for comments from your partner, family, friends, business colleagues, mentors and networks. Say something like, 'I'm thinking of finding a job in *x* sector or *y* organisation. Does that sound like the sort of role where you can picture me?'

When I was offered a role at Whitelion, I asked one of my former partners whether they thought the cause was a good fit for me. They said, 'Steve, helping young kids who are in jail or at risk of getting in trouble with the law – you're a lawyer, for crying out loud. That's a fantastic space for you to be. What's better than someone who's had a great experience with the law being able to help kids who have had such a bad experience with the law?' And I thought, *Yes. That's right.*

People who've known you in your past life may struggle to picture you being passionate about any form of saving the world. But if you cast the net wide enough and speak to enough people who know you, you'll be surprised how the responses start to align. People who've known you in a particular role will often ask you why you want to waste your time in a different sector. Be ready for negative responses to your test-driving. I felt a bit deflated when some people would say, 'Oh, really? The charity sector is just so inefficient. Go back to work as a lawyer, Steve, and donate some money to them.'

I parked that and said, 'Thanks very much for your thoughts.' Then I made a note on my networking spreadsheet (see chapter 8) and realised that not everyone's going to think that what I'm doing is worthwhile. But I still valued their opinion. It was another piece of reflection from people who knew me, just to plug into the equation. Not everyone's going to support you on this journey. You're going to find people who think you're wasting your time. Take their reflections and come to your own conclusions.

KEEP AN EYE OUT FOR THE UNKNOWN PERFECT CAUSE

Does a perfect cause exist, but you don't know about it? In this chapter, I've talked about looking at what you get upset about in the newspaper, along with other options, and whether your friends and colleagues think a particular cause is a good match for you. But now you may need to do some further research on the sector, specifically on organisations and areas, just to make sure that you haven't missed a worthy cause that fires you up. A good place to start is the website for the Australian Charities and Not-for-Profits Commission (ACNC – acnc.gov.au). It shows which causes each charity supports, as well as some basic financial information.

If you're thinking about an international aid organisation based in Australia, the Australian Council for International Development (ACFID) website (acfid.asn.au) provides useful information about those organisations, including their size by revenue.

Other information sources are peak sector organisations – for example, Philanthropy Australia (philanthropy.org.au) and Pro Bono Australia (probonoaustralia.com.au). These organisations have a good handle on what the key contemporary social issues are, and which NFPs are doing a good job addressing those causes. You can study their websites and subscribe to their free online publications.

I also met with the chair and CEO of *The Big Issue*, a newspaper you can buy around Australia (and around the world), sold by homeless people who get 50 per cent of the cost of every copy they sell. But, more importantly in the context of trying to find my perfect cause, *The Big Issue* leaders each gave me powerful insights into where the particular areas of need were in Melbourne and, more broadly, in Australia at the time I was looking. Even simply reading *The Big Issue* will give you an idea of what's going on around your town – and it's a good cause to support.

Finally, radio talkback shows often have informative segments highlighting a particular cause. I usually know the NFPs featured on the radio, but occasionally I hear about a new one to add to my knowledge base.

Since switching sectors, over the years I have done several radio interviews, usually talking about my passion for supporting people facing disadvantage and what my NFP at the time was trying to do to help in that area. So hopefully I was doing my bit to, in turn, encourage people to get involved in the sector.

This final step is important to ensure that you and your contacts haven't missed a potential cause. It also helps to further refine your knowledge and thinking.

Learning about the wide variety of causes supported by Australian NFP organisations was really helpful to me. It opened my eyes to causes I hadn't even been aware of and it helped me better understand the overall sector I was about to enter.

Make the switch

Start doing some research on the areas of interest covered by the NFP sector.

Pick an organisation's website and start there. Review aspects such as its recent annual reports, the About Us section (which usually includes information on the CEO, board and executive team), and the organisation's vision and mission.

Keep abreast of current areas of need, read the papers, listen to the radio and talk to people in the sector. Networking has many benefits, including providing the opportunity to talk to those people who can fill in the gaps as to which cause out there is right for you.

I enjoy learning about the people who are running these organisations. For me, these conversations are where you get a lot of the juice – after reading about what some of these people have done and thinking, *Wow, that's inspiring. What a great cause. I should put that organisation on my list to talk to down the track.*

Sit back and reflect on what you feel could be the best cause for you, what input you've had from your colleagues and what else you have learnt. If you haven't quite got to narrowing down your top cause yet, make a list of your top three. Shop them around with your colleagues to see if they think one in particular is the best.

The next step is exploring job possibilities with organisations working for your preferred cause, which I discuss in detail in chapter 9. If you've got a list of three causes, and you can't get a role in your number one, but you're kind of happy with number two, then it's all right. This gives you flexibility later on to find a job in one of your top three causes. I was pretty keen to work with youth facing disadvantage, and I've been lucky that basically everything I've been involved with since has provided support to that cause.

Give the process some time. Wait until things emerge. If you're not quite sure, and you're an intuitive type of person, you might want to just wait and see which cause sticks with you. If you're a methodical type of person, try ranking them. Put a number against the cause and compare it to all other causes. Is it a six, seven or eight out of ten? Is it a ten out of ten? Find some way of working out what matters.

As part of that process, when you are trying to analyse your own thoughts, consider again some questions from this chapter that will help you get to that outcome. To recap, they are:

- Have you made donations to any charities over the years? Which ones?

- Which TV news item or coverage on one of the public affairs shows often fires you up?

- What about the movies? Do the ones about the kids dying of cancer particularly move you?

- Which charity would you consider giving up your precious time to support as a volunteer without getting paid?

Look for clues in your life that will lead you back to your passions and causes. Use the time while you're still in the corporate sector to get involved with volunteering. Test it out now.

Now you've got an insight into the things that really get the fire going in your belly. Follow those passions through to find the organisations and people working in those areas. If you do that, you're going to end up working in an organisation that gets you jumping out of bed in the morning.

WRAP UP

To get to your ideal position, you've worked through the newspaper test. You've test-driven a cause you've landed on with people who know you. You've also done some research to make sure no gaping holes exist in your knowledge of organisations and their causes. You've looked at everything possible out there to uncover the perfect cause for you. By doing all this, you're giving yourself the best chance that, when you make the move, it's going to be the right move for you.

Of course, what you do isn't the only thing that's important. How you do it is also a factor. In the next chapter, I outline all your choices about how you can enter the NFP sector.

SEVEN

How do you like to work?

Sure, you only have one life. But one of the joys of switching is that you can experience something different during that life.

By this stage in the process, you should have spent time considering what you like doing, what transferable skills you have and what cause you're passionate about. Now it's time to focus on how you like to work, and how you might best contribute to the sector. What is the best environment for you? What sort of role do you imagine you'll have in the organisation? Will you be a leader, a senior executive or a CEO? Or will you be somewhere in the middle ranks? Will you bring in specialist skills? Will you be full-time or part-time, and in a short-term or longer-term role? Will you stay for a couple of months or several years? Would you prefer a larger well-established organisation or a smaller grassroots one? Maybe a start-up? And what about alternative not-for-profit (NFP) roles – such as international NFPs; philanthropic foundations; environmental, social and governance (ESG) roles in a company; and consultancy roles to the sector?

As well as doing more purposeful work, I was keen to try working for a small organisation, and maybe even a four-day week if possible. I ended up spending many special Fridays with my elderly mother before she died – something that would not have been possible during my hectic corporate career. Here's your chance to work the way you'd like to.

You may not end up where you start looking, but the framework I provide in this chapter will help. Keep an open mind.

START AT THE TOP – OR WORK YOUR WAY UP?

What sort of role do you want to have when you move to the NFP sector – executive, specialist, HR or IT, board member or volunteer? As in the corporate world, a huge variety of roles is available. I knew I wanted to start as a senior executive or CEO, so I would have some influence with my seniority through the leadership team or board. At this stage of my career, I didn't want to be a board member or a volunteer, and nor did I want to be wallowing in middle management. If you are transitioning with specialist skills and don't particularly aspire to leadership, seniority may not be as important to you. But even if you do want a leadership position, as I did,

Don't waste time chasing roles that are not the right fit for you, that you have little realistic chance of winning or that will not bring you the happiness and fulfilment that you seek.

my advice is that it's better to get into the sector and work your way up, rather than wait to be offered the senior level job that you think you deserve.

You're travelling a road less travelled. Not many people have successfully transitioned from corporate to the NFP sector. So you need to be strategic about this. Don't waste time chasing roles that are not the right fit for you, that you have little realistic chance of winning or that will not bring you the happiness and fulfilment that you seek. That will not be good for you – and may also do more harm than good at that organisation.

I received lots of advice about what kind of role in the sector might be best for me to start with. Much of the advice was contradictory. Based on the senior executive roles that I've had over the last eight years (including three as a CEO), I've distilled the best advice into this chapter.

A couple of coffee buddies adopted the 'beggars can't be choosers' approach and said that I should accept any NFP job that I was offered, and then work up from there. Others suggested I use my specialist skills as a mergers and acquisitions lawyer to get in the door in a legal capacity, and then move to a leadership role. This did make sense, because ongoing talk in the sector focused on the need for mergers and consolidation. And using any specialist skills you have is certainly one way to switch to the sector – for example, IT skills developed in the business world are transferable to the NFP sector (as discussed in chapter 5). However, as it turned out, I didn't have to take a legal role as my first job.

As well as suggestions to transition as a lawyer, I also received advice to begin as the CEO of a large organisation. Others suggested starting with a small organisation and working towards a larger one.

I had approached many senior corporate executives because of their connections with the NFP world – such as being chairs or directors of charities. As a senior lawyer, I'd been advising their corporate boards in the boardroom for many years. Several of those who knew my high-end business background said that I should 'settle for nothing less than a CEO role and preferably with one of the large national NFPs'. They confidently made assertions to me along the lines of, 'You're a senior guy. Clearly you're just going to be the CEO.' These were very flattering, but not very realistic. Moving straight from a senior executive role in a corporate organisation to a CEO role in an NFP organisation is already so difficult, with too much of a learning curve. So I didn't think I'd start in the corner office. I expected I'd have to work my way up and learn about the sector with humility. Those corporate executives didn't think that would be necessary. As it turned out, they were wrong and I was right. Even if your end goal is leadership, be ready to take a step down first – even if it's not a big step.

The vast majority of my mentors and coffee buddies also said they expected I would fit in best at a larger organisation, because I'd come from one. Notwithstanding that, I've enjoyed being the CEO of mid-sized charities, leading smaller teams delivering services. By mid-sized, I mean a charity such as SecondBite, where as CEO I have about 100 staff around the country and annual revenue of just over $10 million. Doxa Youth Foundation had annual revenue of around $5 million and about 60 staff. Similar to SecondBite, Doxa also had several hundred volunteers. Although I wasn't CEO at Whitelion, as chief operating officer there I had responsibility for 140 staff with $10 million annual revenue. And as head of Australian operations at Save the Children, I had responsibility for 600 staff nationally, with $27 million annual revenue. By comparison, the team I led at Thrive by Five was very small, given that we focused on advocacy rather than delivering programs. Based on those roles, I realise that to date I have been happiest leading a decent-sized team.

Of course, your preference for the type of position you're aiming for should also take into account your partner's views, and your feelings about fundraising.

CONSIDERING YOUR FINANCES AND YOUR PARTNER

As well as the other issues mentioned in this chapter, you should also consider your own financial position and the views of your partner (if you have one). If the lives (or finances) of other family members will also be affected by you switching to the NFP sector, their views may be relevant too.

Your partner's attitude to your transition, in particular their support or otherwise, can be an important factor in its success.

If you've not yet reached financial independence and still need to work to live or to build your retirement nest egg, a key factor in the role you choose will be the salary package. Even though charities can offer tax advantages not available in the corporate world (which increase

Your partner's attitude to your transition, in particular their support or otherwise, can be an important factor in its success.

your 'real' salary), this need for a salary will affect aspects such as the seniority of the position you seek, the size of the organisation, the duration of the role and the weekly hours of work.

It may be that, after consideration of your finances and/or discussions with your partner and perhaps other family members, you decide you are not quite ready to switch yet. In that case, you can start planning now for a future transition, using the suggestions in this book. If you don't feel you can afford to switch yet, perhaps it's a matter of seeing how you can reduce the expenses in your life, or put aside some money now to cover the likelihood of a lesser salary later. Or maybe considering one of the other NFP-related options discussed at the end of this chapter makes more sense. Or maybe you stay in the corporate sector, but use your higher salary and business contacts to support your chosen cause through donations and/or advocacy. You can make a positive contribution to your community in so many ways.

FEELINGS ABOUT FUNDRAISING

Asking for money is usually a big part of life in a small charity. Your business networks may be of interest to an NFP for this reason. In most smaller NFPs, getting money is part of the job for the senior executives and a huge part of the job for the CEO. So if you didn't like asking for money, choose your role and NFP option accordingly.

Make the switch
Consider what sort of tenure would suit your aspirations and life goals. Draw up a table with headings that reflect the issues discussed so far in this chapter – the type of role, responsibilities, and size and location of organisation. Put a ranking from one to ten against each of the factors, with one being the least important to you and ten being the most important. Using that table, and knowing how you like to work, can you get some insights about the best way for you to make your unique contribution?

SHORT- OR LONGER-TERM TENURE?

Are you looking for a short-term role or something longer term? Are you going to work for three to six months with time off in between, or do you want a second career lasting five years? Perhaps you're switching earlier in your career and see yourself working for another 20 years or more. Given the work involved in transitioning, a minimum two-year role makes sense to me. If you want a senior executive role, the role will normally be for around three years initially, while lower level roles might be for shorter periods. In my experience, the NFP sector has higher turnover than the corporate world. And many roles are for a finite term, as some of mine have been, due to their contract nature or fundraising limitations. Don't be surprised if you end up in a shorter-term role than you had initially expected.

You need to be realistic. If you're in your twenties or thirties, you might decide that this will be your career for the next 20 or 30 years. If you're in

What's important is that you make a positive difference, for both the organisation and the people you serve. The time period you stay for is less important.

your sixties, this might be your one last gig before you retire. One senior NFP colleague said to me, 'Two years is enough to make a difference.' She had come from the corporate sector and, after doing a great job for three years, left the NFP world to work in government at a senior executive level. Of course, the longer you stay, the greater – and more lasting – the difference you make is likely to be.

Certain sectors of the NFP world can be emotionally draining. Working in domestic violence or children's cancer are two obvious examples. If your passion is in an emotionally demanding area, consider the term of your engagement even more carefully. Sometimes the work can take a toll and be more exhausting than you expect.

My roles over the last eight years have actually turned out to be more short term than I had originally anticipated. They have been for one to two years, and generally involving change management. What's important is that you make a positive difference, for both the organisation and the people you serve. The time period you stay for is less important.

Although you might not like the idea of a shorter-term role, as long as you focus on making an impact during the time that you're in it, it doesn't matter if it's only a year or two. Hopefully you will continue to learn about the NFP sector, including building your subject matter expertise. This will equip you well for the next stepping stone. I am a curious person and have relished my learning journey in the sector. When I was working at Whitelion, I would often hear about young people my staff were working with in youth justice who had experienced terrible family lives as young children. When I was at Thrive by Five, I had the opportunity to learn in much more detail about the critical importance of the early years in a child's development. It helped me to better understand the connection between the young people in youth detention and what they had gone through in their early years.

I would add a caution regarding short-term visits to the NFP world. You do not want to be seen as a corporate saviour who rides in on their white charger to 'fix the problems' of an NFP before riding off into the distance, having done more harm than good. In the context of writing this book, one of my NFP CEO friends said to me, 'Steve, watch out for those do-gooder corporate types. They think they can come in for a short time and fix an organisation and then go back to the corporate sector, leaving behind a trail of destruction. If you're going to encourage people to come in, make sure that doesn't happen'. Enough said.

Make the switch

You might want a longer-term gig, but struggle to get one. If that's the case, consider accepting a short-term role and taking it from there. While I was working with Whitelion and Save the Children, in both cases I was employed for an initial contract term but that was extended more than once in each organisation. The sector often works on limited funding without knowing whether ongoing funding will be available for a role. Many employment contracts are 'subject to funding' – meaning that, if the relevant funding dries up, you might be out of a job through no fault of your own. It's a challenge that you may come across but, even if you do, at least you've got your foot in the door. Keep your mind open to roles that are 'subject to funding'.

SMALL OR LARGE ORGANISATION?
SMALL OR LARGE CHALLENGE?

Preferring a small or larger organisation is a tricky decision, and one I still grapple with. Most of my mentors thought I'd be going for a large organisation, but I've enjoyed working in small- to medium-sized ones more than I had expected.

NFPs in Australia can be divided very roughly as follows (with a few examples given):

- Extra-large international NGOs – examples include World Vision, Save the Children, Oxfam, CARE, Plan International, Red Cross, UNICEF and WWF. (The term 'NGO' – non-governmental organisation – is often used for an NFP that is addressing more widespread issues, often operating internationally.)

- Large/national NFPs – such as Anglicare, St Vincent de Paul, The Smith Family, Mission Australia, Life Without Barriers and Brotherhood of St. Laurence.

- Small and single-state NFPs ($0 to $10 million) – examples include Whitelion, Reach Foundation, Lighthouse Foundation and Kids Under Cover.

The pros and cons of large and small NFPs are highly subjective, and will depend in part on the kind of organisation you're used to, along with what you're looking for from your NFP work. In this section, I can only share some of my general thoughts. Large NFPs are likely to be better resourced, you're less likely to have to be a 'jack-of-all-trades', and they are likely to have greater impact, possibly part of global change. The downside is that they can become bureaucratic and you can feel removed from the cause.

With smaller NFPs, you're likely to see increased focus on teamwork and a strong sense of purpose. The downside includes being constantly under-resourced.

One of my coffee buddies predicted that I would miss the 'sheltered workshop' of a large law firm. His conclusion was that I should work in a large, well-resourced NFP organisation, with similar elements to my old law firm. Others told me about the joy of working with a small, passionate organisation.

I'm embarrassed to admit that I did miss some of the luxuries of a big law firm, such as the wonderful admin support services, the photocopying team, the tea lady (well, not since the 1990s!), the receptionists and all the other support staff. Although all of that was wonderful, the benefits of being in an organisation with a clear purpose to try to improve people's lives outweighed any negatives of losing the comforts of a corporate role.

One CEO of an international aid NGO warned me about being 'up to your neck in alligators' in a small NFP. What he was getting at is that the CEO of a small NFP can spend a lot of time just dealing with bushfires: Is there enough money to pay the staff next month? These two staff members have been fighting and don't want to sit together any more. The key funder has indicated

Some wonderful aspects also emerge when working in a small NFP with a committed team of passionate people pulling together to change lives.

funding cuts might be coming next month. And so on. And the CEO is often dealing with these myriad challenges without the help of an in-house HR person. But some wonderful aspects also emerge when working in a small NFP with a committed team of passionate people pulling together to change lives. I loved my two years as CEO at Doxa, where a small but dedicated team achieved great outcomes.

Most of my corporate mentors expected that I would end up working as a senior executive in a large NFP. But that was not the case with Mark Watt from Whitelion, who turned out to be a better judge of my potential contribution in the sector than many of my other mentors and even myself. His advice at the start was that a small to mid-size charity would play to my strengths, including my people skills and fundraising skills – and be a welcome change from the bureaucracy of a large organisation, from which I was ready to escape. I think he was right, at least at that early stage in my journey.

And it's not just the size of the organisation you need to consider – it's also the size of the challenge for you within the organisation.

Even organisations of the same size, working for the same cause, may have different focuses in their work. For example, some focus on service delivery, such as Whitelion, working with youth at risk; others do social enterprise, such as Streat, the Melbourne-based hospitality NFP; some specialise in fundraising, such as Variety, the children's charity; and some do advocacy and support work, such as Justice Connect. Choose the one that excites you, based on the guidelines from this section and throughout the book.

Make the switch

To help decide what size organisation is best for you, look through the pros and cons outlined in this section for each type of organisation. Give them each points out of ten, with ten meaning that it matters a lot to you and one meaning that it doesn't matter at all. Reflecting on the numbers, what's becoming clear to you about how you can make your contribution?

OTHER OPTIONS INSIDE AND OUTSIDE THE NFP SECTOR

As well as working for an Australian NFP, you might consider four other options:

1. International NGOs, such as the overseas operations of Save the Children and World Vision. If you want to make a difference on the ground in an African country, for example, you need to explore the options they can give you.

2. The world of philanthropy.

3. An ESG role in a company.

4. Consultant to the sector.

WORKING FOR AN INTERNATIONAL NGO

Many important roles exist in the international NGO sector, and one might suit you. But when I considered those, I ended up coming back to Australia. It was where I wanted to work. Although I've focused on the general area of the Australian NFP sector, literally a whole wide world of other opportunities is out there. During my coffee due diligence journey (see chapter 8), I went through a stage of wanting to end global poverty. I approached parts of my network who were based overseas and had connections internationally with various international NGOs, including overseas contacts from when I worked as a lawyer in New York and in Asia. I grew my overseas NGO network, even to the extent of having the late Sir James Wolfensohn, former President of the World Bank, writing on my behalf to the New York based General Counsel of the World Bank! But I also learned how difficult it would be for me to work overseas. Most Australians working for UN-affiliated organisations were appointed by the Australian government or its diplomatic agencies. For pragmatic reasons, I decided to focus on causes closer to home. It became clear to me that the sector of young people facing disadvantage in Australia was where I wanted to work.

FOCUSING YOUR EFFORTS ON PHILANTHROPY

I have also worked in philanthropy, as the inaugural CEO of Thrive by Five, the early childhood initiative of Andrew and Nicola Forrest's Minderoo Foundation. This was a great opportunity to work in the early childhood area, develop and get board approval of a three-year strategic plan, build a team to deliver it, advocate with government at a federal and state level (including two meetings face to face with Prime Minister Scott Morrison) and work with government agencies and research centres to fund evidence-based programs. Philanthropic funding is obviously a key element of the sector – but for the moment I'm happy to keep closer to the front line, leading a passionate team delivering programs that help people facing disadvantage. If you enjoy leading a team, one of the downsides of philanthropy is that the teams tend to be relatively small, particularly compared to a service-delivery organisation.

MOVING TO AN ESG ROLE

Because at this stage of my life I wanted a complete break from the corporate sector, I didn't really explore the option of working in the growing area of ESG, where environmental, social and governance issues are incorporated into corporate decision-making and investment practice. Having said that, you may wish to explore this option further, as a way of doing good without completely exiting the business world, and without leaving behind the corporate pay packet. You may even be able to switch to working in this area within your existing organisation. Chances are, you already have a 'gut feel' whether this is enough of a switch for you and whether this change will allow you to make the type of contribution you're ready to make. Your networking process will also provide the necessary information and contacts to explore this route further.

ACTING AS A CONSULTANT

In a similar vein to taking on an ESG role, providing consultancy or advisory services to the NFP sector might sound like less of an undertaking, or perhaps more like a stepping stone, to making a difference while still retaining your connection to the business world. Such sector consulting could be provided on your own, or with an existing advisory organisation such as Social Ventures Australia or People for Purpose.

You might be feeling paralysed by all these possibilities. Don't worry. Your networking coffees (which I discuss further in the following chapter) will make the choices clearer. If you think one of these options may be right for you, remember to include questions about that option in subsequent coffee meetings. You'll gradually finesse your questions and develop your own thinking about how you can best contribute to the sector.

Make the switch

Consider whether you might prefer a less typical contribution to the NFP sector. Providing greater detail on the international options is outside the scope of this book, but if working overseas sounds interesting, you will need to do some research on the international NGOs – including their focus areas, annual revenues and comparative size. Refer to the website of the Australian Council for International Development (ACFID – acfid.asn.au) for more information.

What about philanthropy? One mentor told me it would be less exhausting than running an NFP, and not such a radical change from my previous world. I could even keep wearing a suit and tie! But to date I have been happier leading teams of a reasonable size at service-delivery organisations.

If you want to do good from within in the for-profit corporate world, maybe you could be head of ESG somewhere, or even be the battle-hardened corporate adviser to a start-up doing good, or to the sector generally.

But what is right for you? You can discuss these ideas with your coffee mentors.

As you expand your search, keep careful notes because you don't want to lose track of the information you gather. (See the following chapter for the key details of my networking system.)

WRAP UP

This chapter highlights that you have many choices. Before you take the next step, consider what would be ideal for you – including thinking about the type of role, the size of the organisation, the length of your commitment and those other alternatives to the NFP sector.

If you've climbed the corporate ladder, you might not have had to consider your job choices for a while. You may have forgotten you have so many options. Now's your chance to reboot your decision-making. How do you like to work? What form of contribution seems right for you? How exciting to finally have the opportunity to work the way you want!

Talk to your network, especially the headhunters and senior NFP leaders, because they'll often know about potential roles in the sector before they are advertised. Don't forget to talk to your partner as well.

In the next chapter, I cover building and working with this network in much more detail. If, like me, you're a curious person who enjoys spending time with people, this is the fun bit! And even if you're not, the next chapter will make networking a lot easier for you.

EIGHT

Networking

Who would have 171 coffee meetings, mainly with complete strangers, over a 12-month period? And keep notes of each meeting on a detailed spreadsheet?

Well, I did! And here's why ...

This chapter outlines the importance of networking in your transition process. You can't learn everything about the not-for-profit (NFP) sector from a book. So in this chapter I explain why networking is important – maybe even fun! – and how I went about it.

I enjoy meeting people and am a curious person. So I enjoyed the opportunity to talk with a variety of people and learn about the various causes they worked to support. I asked question after question about their NFP career journeys, which helped with my own learning and transition. However, even if you don't like people – and aren't curious – you will still need to do some networking. Sorry.

Building a network has many benefits – including learning about the sector, getting a job and having contacts who can provide ongoing information and support once you're part of the sector. The NFP sector is rapidly changing, so building a group who can provide you with some support along the way is important.

The best time to start networking is as a 'cleanskin' – by this I mean someone who is new to the sector and not aligned to a particular organisation.

Building a network has many benefits – including learning about the sector, getting a job and having contacts who can provide ongoing information and support once you're part of the sector.

Ask people, 'Would you be willing to give me some of your time and advice about coming to work in your sector?' Explain what you're trying to do, and ask them for their thoughts. I found people were very generous with their time if I went in on the basis that I didn't have the answers – but did have enthusiasm, curiosity and an open mind.

In this chapter, I explain how I approached my networking and why it has to be so thorough. I felt that personal networks would not just help me find a job, but also make me more effective once I found one. This is borne out by the research. In 'The social side of performance' (published in *MIT Sloan Management Review*), authors Rob Cross, Thomas Davenport and Susan Cantrell discuss what separates high-performing knowledge workers from their peers. They argue it's not just peer expertise, education and training, or good data sources: 'What really distinguishes high performers from the rest of the pack is their ability to maintain and leverage personal networks.'

The risk of not networking is that your assumptions about the NFP sector go unchallenged. This is known as the 'echo chamber effect', a term coined by Brian Uzzi and Shannon Dunlap in their *Harvard Business Review* article 'How to build your network'. You've got to be aware of this echo chamber effect if your own contexts and those of your network are too similar. The article references a study conducted by Professors Paul Ingram and Michael Morris from the University of Columbia, which looked at whether executives making new contacts would seek out their own type or be more adventurous.

Ingram and Morris arranged a business mixer event using electronic devices that recorded who spent time with whom. The executives were told the idea was to meet as many different people as possible. But the participants formed new ties with others who were most like them – the investment bankers went to talk with the investment bankers, the money marketing execs went to the other marketing executives, and so on. (They also put a tracer on the bartender and he was, by far, the most successful networker of the evening!)

So, as you start your networking process, be aware of your likely tendency to move towards people who are like you – and avoid the temptation to just network with people with whom you feel comfortable.

Some of my discussions with people whom I didn't warm to – perhaps because we had different opinions – turned out to be the most challenging, thought-provoking and useful discussions.

I remember one coffee with the CEO of an organisation working with homeless people. He argued strongly that the biggest community issue was affordable housing – why would I waste my time checking out any other causes, given that they would largely disappear if the big challenge of housing could be fixed? And when the conversation moved to fundraising, he had a strong view that too many NFPs opportunistically chased funds even if it meant that they strayed from their mission (the infamous 'mission drift'). It was quite an aggressive conversation – but I came away with a firm focus that any NFP organisation I led would certainly not succumb to mission drift!

> *The risk of not networking is that your assumptions about the NFP sector go unchallenged.*

I focus on five areas in this chapter:

1. why you can't learn about switching just from a book – and why talking to people is a necessity

2. the various benefits networking can bring – including gathering information (learning and due diligence), road-testing potential roles and finding mentors

3. the three questions for successful NFP networking

4. keeping a record of your networking

5. the advantages of being a 'cleanskin' (that is, new to the sector).

YOU CAN'T LEARN IT ALL FROM A BOOK

You can't learn about the NFP sector, or how you'll switch into it, just from a book. This book will give you guidance and assistance, but you won't be able to transition from the corporate world to the NFP world unless you also talk to people. Now you've decided to pursue a role in the NFP sector, it's time to talk. Get used to caffeine (or decaf, if that's your preference).

Here's my networking story. From early 2014 I spent 12 months meeting with as many people as I could. I wanted to learn as much as possible about the NFP sector – stuff that you can't learn from a book or from online research. And I wanted to build a network of trusted advisers and mentors to support me in my ongoing NFP journey. I started with three questions (see the section 'The three basic questions', later in this chapter), the last one of which is specifically focused on growing your NFP network as quickly as possible.

So how do you start? Start with your contacts in the corporate sector, particularly ones who have connections in the NFP sector. In my case, that was people I knew through business connections but who served as directors or chairs of charities. I also used NFP contacts I met over the years I headed my law firm's charity committee, and worked as a corporate pro bono lawyer and fundraiser. This process works. From not even having a LinkedIn account, within 12 months I had over 1500 LinkedIn connections from that networking.

While on the topic of LinkedIn, I should mention what a great networking tool it is. Among its many benefits, LinkedIn also allows you to learn about someone before meeting them, as well as identifying people in a particular organisation and which of your connections knows them. This enables

LinkedIn's biggest benefit – as a tool you can use to obtain an introduction to someone you would like to meet.

I gained several early learnings from my networking. I hadn't realised how much this sector runs with passion and its heart on its sleeve. I was also surprised at how under-resourced some charities are. (Later on, I was to experience that under-resourcing firsthand, when at one NFP I wasn't sure how we'd be paying the staff salaries the following month.)

I managed to distil a lot of the information from the notes I made in those coffee meetings. Those notes not only helped during my own journey when switching to the NFP sector, but also formed the basis of this book. You'll need your own system for recording what you learn during networking – see 'Keep a record', later in this chapter, for more.

If you're an introvert, you're probably quaking in your boots right now. I realise that some people don't like putting themselves out there with strangers, which is a necessary part of networking. Similarly, many people feel uncomfortable walking into a party of strangers. Personally, I love meeting people and I'm a curious sort of person. So, perhaps unusually for many, I found the whole networking process to be a lot of fun – well, most of the time. If you are more introverted, or even just a

You do need to be a bit brave. Remember – even people-lovers sometimes have to push themselves to network.

little rusty, start by approaching corporate contacts who you know well. You'll feel comfortable talking to them and when they introduce you to their NFP contact, they'll be able to let the contact know about your apprehension. Perhaps they'll also put in a few pointers that will start that conversation off so you're not coming in cold. You do need to be a bit brave. Remember – even people-lovers sometimes have to push themselves to network.

SETTING UP YOUR NETWORKING SYSTEM

Overcoming inertia is easier if you have a good system. So let's discuss in some detail what was involved in the networking system I set up. (I cover how I recorded my learnings from my networking later in this chapter.) I don't want to be accused of teaching grandmother to suck eggs so, if you have developed your own networking system or don't need the detail that follows, feel free to skip over the next few pages.

Successful networkers tend to employ three tactics:

1. Establish personal connections, not just professional ones.

2. Follow through – for example, respond promptly to emails and build trust by doing what you say you're going to do. A good general response rule is at most a 36-hour response time.

3. Actively reciprocate. Networking is a two-way street and, by actively reciprocating, I found I had more information to offer the longer I spent in the NFP sector.

At the start, reciprocating is hard because, while people are helping you, you're not sure what you can offer them, which is how this whole networking deal works. It's not a one-way street. Over time, you'll start picking up things that are useful to people you're talking to – about your impressions of the sector, for example, or something that people are doing to save resources elsewhere that might be valuable to the person you're talking with. By the end of these coffee meetings, I was confident that I was giving as good as I was getting, without betraying any confidences.

Start by asking yourself who in your existing corporate contacts has connections in the NFP world. I started with my own corporate connections from my legal career. I was interested in introductions to the most senior person I could reach in the NFP that I was learning about – the CEO, a senior executive, or maybe a chairperson. If you are bringing specific skills, such as IT skills or HR specialist skills, your focus might be more on who you can meet in the NFP sector who already does this sort of work. And that might be a slightly different approach. It often helps to talk to the person who is working in the role that you want. If you are switching earlier in your career than I did, you may find you have fewer contacts or that they are at a different level than you're aiming for. It doesn't matter – as long as you get started. I wanted to meet people in the higher roles and understand how they were chosen by the board. It was important for me to start my networking at that level in the organisation if I could. Sometimes I couldn't get across to that level, so I'd meet the head of fundraising or some other employee. At World Vision, I met someone quite low in the chain and, through them, got through to more senior people. Work with what you've got.

How the meetings were structured depended on who I was meeting with. If it was with someone who was as talkative as I am, I'd often have to rein them in because I wanted to make the most of my time. But if it was with someone who was a little less effusive and a bit more introverted, I would let them take a running start with an easy question, and

> You may find you have fewer contacts or that they are at a different level than you're aiming for. It doesn't matter – as long as you get started.

then lead up to a more complicated one. Once you get them at ease, you can ask the hard questions. The best advice would often come late in a meeting, when I had built up some trust, and my coffee buddy told me about some stuff-up in their career. That's when you can get some of the best info.

As part of my networking system, I used a few questions to break the ice. How long have you been in the sector? Did you start at this organisation? If you didn't, what's your journey been? Why are you passionate about this area? In the NFP world, these questions usually get things off to a good start. Some people you encounter in the corporate world might be in a job just because they need to pay the mortgage. If you ask why they love their work, you might find the conversation grinds to halt, because frankly they don't love it. But that happens rarely in the NFP world. Usually the people you talk with are in a role they are quite passionate about. Questions about that role will put them at ease and then you can start moving them back to the critical questions. I always bought the coffee, and I always said thank you afterwards and sent a thank you email. (Once you've written up the thank you note once, you can cut and paste it a hundred times, tweaking to suit that particular person.)

I would generally connect with people via email if the introducer was willing to send an email and copy me in on it. That was the most efficient way.

Some people preferred to send the first email without me being party to it, and I respected that. They'd often come back and say something like, 'Okay, I've been in touch with Mary and she's happy to speak with you. Here's her email, here's her phone number.' I'd take whatever lead I was given that way. You don't want to be too pushy. But I can't think of an example where I was introduced to someone who then wouldn't speak with me. Sometimes people are very busy, but busy people will still normally send you an invitation for a meeting of around 45 minutes. For someone who was a bit more relaxed, it was an hour or so. Meeting for 45 to 60 minutes is enough. Sometimes you get on like a house on fire and go past the hour, but I felt that I should let them out of it within 60 minutes if possible.

As I've mentioned, the introduction from the person you know to a new contact can take various forms. In my interactions, these included:

1. Joint email (from the referrer to the contact, copying me in) – this is the most efficient.

2. Separate email or phone call (from referrer to contact, without me) – this is probably fairer to the contact because it allows an easy decline, but does add an extra step for you.

3. Referrer simply giving you the contact's mobile number or email address – this was quite common when the referrer was a particularly busy or well-known person. Although very efficient, I sometimes felt awkward reaching out to the contact without any apparent commentary or imprimatur from the referrer.

Even if I thought a contact offered to me might not be very helpful, I always followed it up. If you've asked a friend or referrer for an introduction, saying

'No, thanks' because the contact offered doesn't seem important enough or you're no longer interested just seems bad form.

Overall, my networking system involved the following key elements:

1. Identify the contact (and work out with the referrer who will make first contact).

2. Arrange the meeting, making it easy for the contact to say yes – through, for example, venue choice (I usually offered 'at your office or a cafe nearby'), or timing options (offer busy people a few times; PAs usually prefer free choice).

3. Hold the meeting, checking that taking notes is okay, and focusing on the three questions I cover later in this chapter.

4. After the meeting, review and fine-tune your notes – make a record of any themes that are consistent or conflict with other advice to date, along with any homework or follow-up required of you.

5. Deal with any follow-up items, including following up with any introductions offered, diarising a further meeting with the referrer, or sending through details of a media article or report you promised.

6. Send a thank you email (I used a template).

7. Keep in touch regularly.

What about networking remotely, where you can't meet face to face? You will notice that this networking process is very much about meetings in person. In the previous chapter, I discuss other NFP options such as with an overseas organisation, which is something I explored briefly. In these cases (and others, such as during covid times), you may need to begin the networking process by phone or Zoom-style video calls. But nothing beats a face-to-face meeting if you can manage it.

Sometimes the networking process seems to drag on and on, without any specific job prospect arising. After several months of coffees, I asked my career coach, the extraordinary Bill Cowan, 'Is this ever going to end?' It took me about 12 months to get my first role. Now that you have this book in your hands, you can do it a lot more efficiently than I did. But I wouldn't shortcut the process, because while you are making these contacts and speaking to these people, while you're still the cleanskin and they're trying to help you as someone who's not in the sector, you have your best opportunities. You've got to get people to sit down and give you their time. Once you're in the sector and another worker just like them, you're two very busy people who'll be lucky to get a 30-minute coffee together, and you won't receive the same sort of benefits. Don't rush the process. Enjoy the fact that it's taking a while.

You'll face barriers like I did with my wife, who would say to me, 'Will you please ask your career coach how many more coffees you're going to have before you get a job? I married you for better, for worse, but not for lunch!' But my coach couldn't answer that because we didn't know. How long does it take to network effectively? It depends on all sorts of things – the environment, the job market, whether a fit is available for your particular area. As a general rule, I've been told that in 12 to 18 months you should have a gig. Initially, I was just talking to people, trying to build up my knowledge, and work out whether the NFP sector was right for me. And then during the networking process, I realised that I really wanted a job in the sector, and to start making a difference. From when I started to really focus on getting a job, it took me about eight months. You may have already decided before reading this book that you want to get a job in the sector. Networking is one way of confirming your interest.

Make the switch

So now you can get underway. Ask yourself who in your existing corporate contacts has connections in the NFP world. And then it's a matter of following the networking system I've outlined in this section – adjusted as you feel appropriate for your own circumstances, so that you can be genuine. It has to feel right for you.

NETWORKING FOR THREE BENEFITS

The three main benefits of networking are:

1. learning about the sector

2. road-testing potential roles

3. finding mentors.

Networking provides a unique opportunity to learn about the sector, and the wide variety of causes encompassed within it, from your own personal perspective. I call this your due diligence. When I was a lawyer and clients were thinking of investing in a business, we would spend a lot of time researching and understanding the industry sector, the risks if the client invested into that sector, how to mitigate those risks and who the important players were. In many ways, those concepts of due diligence, which come from a legal context, can apply here as you start your foray into the NFP world.

> *Networking provides a unique opportunity to learn about the sector, and the wide variety of causes encompassed within it, from your own personal perspective. I call this your due diligence.*

As you learn more, you can start road-testing with the people you meet your ideas about where you might fit into the sector. You'll also build a valuable network for the future – for both before and after you start working in the sector. Note that I didn't include finding a job as a specific outcome of networking. As the old saying goes, 'Ask for a job and you'll get advice; ask for advice and you'll get a job'. Having said that, you should include headhunters in your network. Some specialise in NFP recruitment, and they can provide invaluable advice (and potentially a job, once you're on their list).

I found that my coffee buddies would often include an NFP executive recruitment specialist when I asked them for their proposed introductions (see 'The three basic questions', later in this chapter). The more often a particular name arose, the more likely they were to be a useful contact. If you don't start hearing the names of headhunters in your early coffee meetings, you can raise the topic.

My networking focused on making sure that I was covering all three of these areas of learning about the sector, road-testing potential roles and finding mentors.

Networking was the subject of 'Learning the art of meeting for coffee leads to roles' (published in *The Australian Financial Review*) by Katie Lahey, then executive chair of headhunter firm Korn Ferry Australasia. Lahey focused on non-executive director roles in the article, but her points also apply to NFP executive roles. Her advice was to first practise your pitch. Starting a conversation with, 'I'm thinking of slowing down, and thought a board career might offer flexibility' is not a good start! As Lahey notes, 'Your exposure to boards throughout your executive career, coupled with your desire to remain in the business world, working on a diverse portfolio of board and advisory roles is a more constructive way to start a conversation.' The same is true of the conversations you have over coffee on your NFP switching journey.

When you're networking and asking questions, you need to be careful about how you phrase them. The context of how you ask those questions is important. If you go in and say, 'I'm thinking about someday doing something useful and maybe I thought I could do some good in the NFP sector,' the person you're sitting down with isn't going to be terribly inspired. What worked for me was saying, 'I've been working in the corporate world for a long time and I think I've got some skills that I can contribute in your sector. I understand I'm at the bottom of the learning curve and I would really appreciate some help. Would you possibly be willing to give me 30 minutes of your time?' That approach worked well for me to get the benefits of NFP networking at all three levels. It gave me a reason to explain that I was trying to learn and do my due diligence. It gave me an opening to explain my potential, using those skills that I touched on in that little pitch I just mentioned. And if I was willing to be vulnerable like that in a conversation, the other person was much more likely to say, 'You know what, I could actually be your mentor. Let's talk.'

Lahey also says that the first 20 minutes are the most important that you can invest in networking. Think about the location where you're going to meet. I was mainly interested in NFPs located in Victoria, but I did look at some interstate-based organisations. Do your research on the organisation. Pick your moment, timing-wise. Saying you want to find a job in the next week and you've just left your old job last week is going to say a lot about you (and not in a good way). Identify who will be the most useful people from your networking meetings. It comes down to how some people who you're referred to are more beneficial than others, and it makes sense to put the effort into those who you think will help you, without wanting to sound too opportunistic.

This might seem a little cold-blooded and calculating but, at the end of the day, you are asking these people for help, so that in turn you can help others.

Once you have been offered an NFP role, your (growing) network can be a useful source of due diligence regarding the quality (or otherwise) of your potential employer.

When I was a lawyer in the corporate world, I acted for various listed investment companies. One such client never invested in a company without meeting the CEO and board face to face and speaking to them about their vision. Of course, the client also crunched the numbers. But if you speak to someone about their organisation, ask the right questions – such as, 'Is there anything else that perhaps isn't as good as you'd like it to be about your organisation?' Questions like that can start showing up issues that may not have come over in the first flush when the person was trying to tell you about the good things about their organisation and why you should come to the sector. Face-to-face interrogation is the most useful technique. But you still have to do your research online, talk to other people, look at annual reports that are available publicly and so on.

Which of the three levels you emphasise will depend on your personal circumstances. For example, I added a lot of people to my contact list. My focus was very much about building my network and mentors, but I didn't do much road-testing of potential roles. I know of people who use this networking process to focus more on learning about specific areas of the sector and what jobs are available. This process is quite flexible. What level you decide to focus on will depend on where you are in the journey and your own personality.

Regardless of the outcome you focus on during a particular networking meeting, which of the three benefits you receive will differ from meeting to meeting. One person will be able to shed more light on the due diligence aspect, while another person might shed more light on the roles available and the demands of those roles. Be aware of which of the three benefits you are receiving from a particular meeting or person. If someone gives great advice on a particular area but doesn't add much information on your other two areas, you need to fill in those gaps somehow. I had these three benefits of networking in the back of my mind when I was asking my three basic questions (see the following section). The answers to these questions will tend to come out through the natural course of conversation, provided you keep them in mind.

As you increase your network, you'll find that the individual threads do start to weave an extraordinary fabric. Everyone will have their own contribution. As you start looking back at what you've learned, you will generally have covered off all those three levels. As you progress and review your notes, think about where you are still lacking input and respond to that by changing the focus as your meetings progress. As my networking progressed, I did tend to focus more on the second level of road-testing potential roles.

Conversations can drift and become a little unfocused, especially when you like someone. The purpose of having these three levels in the back of your mind is to maintain that focus. To keep on track, have some segue-type comments in mind – for example:

- 'Can I ask you again about the roles?'

- 'I've lost my train of thought; could we come back to the way that this organisation gets funded?'

- 'Can you remind me again what the organisational structure is for your organisation?'

- 'You've given me some great advice; did you have someone who gave you advice?'

Make the switch

In order to make the most of your coffee meeting and to show respect for the other person's time, ensure you're well prepared for the meeting – including doing some research about the other person and their organisation, and what you hope to get out of the meeting. As well as what's available through LinkedIn, worthwhile background information is also available on the internet – about the individual, as well as their organisation. Look at the organisation website and annual reports.

When you get their name from a contact, ask for a little bit of detail and write it down, which will give you a head start when you do meet them – so you can say, for example, 'Janet told me you worked together at Save the Children. Can you tell me about the time you spent in the Northern Territory?'

THE THREE BASIC QUESTIONS

The three questions I asked at every coffee meeting (and the reasons for them) were:

1. *Is there a place for me in the sector?* If the answer to this first question is no, progressing to the next two questions is pointless. Fortunately, for me, that never happened – although some people were less enthusiastic than others about how useful I might be! I'm sure most people you meet with will be able to identify at least some sort of role where your skills can be used.

2. *What weaknesses will I need to address?* I often had to push for an honest answer to this question, because people usually don't want to find fault or hurt your feelings – particularly some of the gentler NFP types. But it was a useful question, and honest answers often led to a good discussion.

3. *Would you be willing to introduce me to two more people in the NFP sector?* From names arising during the conversation, who these two people might be was usually obvious, but sometimes it was more random. Often I was cheeky enough to push for three or four names. The answers coming from this question formed the basis of the huge growth in my LinkedIn connections in a short time.

One important outcome of this third question is that it requires the new contact to take some action after the meeting, even if it is only a couple of phone calls or emails. This makes it more likely that they will remember who you are, and what you are doing. Later in my journey, when I was on the other side and having coffees with prospective switchers, I certainly found that to be the case. It is very easy to have a coffee, dish out advice, do nothing else – and then forget the person! What a shameful admission to make. Avoid being forgotten when you seek advice from someone by making yourself memorable – ideally through leaving them with a little homework to do.

The three questions look simple, but they resulted in answers that varied greatly, not just in their content, but also in the perspective from which they were given. Often they would lead to a discussion about what I was trying to achieve and, almost as often, about what my new friend on the other side of the table was trying to achieve with their life.

As I've outlined, the third objective of this networking is to find trusted mentors, people who will stand beside you on the journey. Through the networking process, I developed relationships with about ten key mentors, who I catch up with every six months or so. I found about 30 other mentors who are important but not key mentors, and I catch up with them every 12 to 18 months.

Avoid being forgotten when you seek advice from someone by making yourself memorable – ideally through leaving them with a little homework to do.

As discussed earlier, I started the process by meeting with people I knew from the corporate world, but who had strong NFP involvement – such as ex–Macquarie banker Simon McKeon and Ian Carson of SecondBite fame, both of whom have been great mentors. But over time I added mentors who had been in the NFP sector for their entire working lives.

With this rich panel of wisdom to draw from, whenever an issue arises I can call a mentor, tell them what I am struggling with, and ask for their advice. And I can sometimes help them with an issue they are dealing with, even though they have been in the sector for longer. That exchange is a rewarding part of the process.

During the networking meetings, I took notes and wrote down names and anything that was worthwhile – some learnings I hadn't thought of, roles I hadn't thought would be relevant for me, and the details of people referred to me as possible mentors.

These three tried and true questions work. Though simple, I found them to be magic. They can be challenging for your new coffee buddy but they get to the nub of the issues you need to resolve. You're asking for someone to open up their networks, which is something you wouldn't do until you've built some sense of trust with them.

You might think that this sounds artificial or exploitive. In the article by Cross, Davenport and Cantrell I refer to at the start of this chapter, their advice is to 'focus on building deeper relationships that will be mutually beneficial over time'. Building networks is too important to leave to chance. Do the work and reap the rewards. If these questions seem too simple, don't worry, they're just a starting point. Once you get underway and the conversation starts up, other questions are sure to flow both ways as the other person starts to take an interest in what you're trying to do. I found the three basic questions, though simple, led to very thought-provoking discussions.

As the meeting went along, we would usually have a bit of a chat about their sector and about my background in the corporate sector. I had been a lawyer for all those years and had enjoyed it. By the time you've done this many times, asking these questions comes pretty smoothly – along the lines of, 'I've been in the corporate sector, here's my background, here's what I want to do. Can you tell me a bit about your background?' and then question one, two and three. And remember – more listening and less talking!

Tell your coffee buddy that you're asking everyone you meet these three questions. Telling them this adds weight to the questions. If you were the one being asked the questions, you'd want to make sure your answers were as helpful – or more so! – than the answers others are providing.

Make the switch

You may meet with someone who has a negative attitude towards your plan to transition. Perhaps they see you as a bossy corporate refugee coming to save the NFP sector. If that happens, don't be deterred from your vision, just learn what you can. Use your three questions if you can, still finding out as much information as possible. You may only learn that you don't want to be like that person, or to work in that area – but this is still good insight. And, anyway, the experience provides good practice for answering future doubters and being ready for the next meeting.

KEEP A RECORD

Earlier in this chapter, I mentioned the importance of keeping a record of your networking. This network information spreadsheet (by whatever name you use) provides a framework for your networking system and collects in one place all the advice you receive.

As part of my networking system, I set a target number of five coffee meetings each week, with a minimum of two. This may not seem difficult, but wait until it's week 52 and you're over it! Another focus of my system was to keep a record of key information – answers to the three basic questions, for example, along with advice and important quotes. This was my gold. I had a separate backup for this record, because I knew that if I lost it, I was going to be in a bit of strife. To this day, I still go back to my networking information spreadsheet from time to time – for example, I used it as research for this book.

Along with the key information, the spreadsheet also recorded thank you notes sent, actions taken and follow-ups required – for example, if they'd suggested that we have a subsequent meeting. The provided figure shows a section of my networking spreadsheet, highlighting the kind of information I included.

Once you have successfully switched into the sector, you can also use your record system to ensure that you keep in touch with your wider list of contacts, including letting them know of any subsequent job changes.

I looked for common themes in the answers to my three questions, and having all my notes together in an accessible form helped when I periodically reviewed where I was at during the 12 months.

Having a proven system makes the networking process easier for you. You don't have to gird your loins for each meeting, work out what questions you should ask and make sure you don't forget really important things. And you keep track of insights gained and contacts made along the way. Without my system, I would have struggled with the challenges of inertia and laziness.

Section from networking information spreadsheet

DATE	NAME	CLASSIFICATION	REFERRED BY	COMMENTS	SUGGESTED REFERRALS/ TO MEET	ACTION/ TO MEET
23/08/2021	Kylie Fernando	Corporate	Self/ corporate contact	1 Good contact in youth sector 2 Suggested aiming for senior exec role in NFP	• Nellie Hanson (PWC partner, chair of youth charity) • Lucy Gordon (World Vision exec)	• N. Hanson • L. Gordon
23/08/2021	Michael Stone	Headhunter, referral	Tamara Hills (former client)	1 Mentioned Red Cross state manager role 2 Offered to review CV 3 Suggested monitoring ethicaljobs.com.au	• Kumari Mason (Save the Children exec) • Simon Bruce (philanthropy)	• K. Mason • S. Bruce • Monitor job sites • Send draft CV
24/08/2021	Nellie Hanson	NFP chair, corporate background, referral	Kylie Fernando	1 Will miss comfort of big law firm 2 Involve spouse on journey 3 I mentioned book *Twenty Good Summers*	• Sally Brown (Whitelion exec) • Fatima Singh (NFP CEO)	• S. Brown • F. Singh • Send details of *Twenty Good Summers* by Martin Hawes • Send update and thank you to K. Fernando

DATE	NAME	CLASSIFICATION	REFERRED BY	COMMENTS	SUGGESTED REFERRALS/ TO MEET	ACTION/ TO MEET
24/08/2021	Lucy Gordon	NFP – World Vision exec, referral	Kylie Fernando	1 Offer to volunteer with NFP in my preferred area 2 Be patient	• Robert Stevens (NFP CEO) • Jack Strapp (NFP, program lead)	• R. Stevens • J. Strapp • Send update and thank you to K. Fernando
27/08/2021	Simon Bruce	NFP exec, philanthropic foundation	Mike Stone	1 No specific advice 2 Seems well connected	• Jane Trimble (headhunter)	• J. Trimble • Send update and thank you to M. Stone

A big part of why I think networking is fun is the constant interaction with people whom I like and respect. The NFP sector can be so generous. Your meetings are very different from the kinds of coffee meetings you might have in the business world, which are usually much more transactional. What's in it for you and for me? In the people-centric NFP sector, the relationship side builds much more quickly.

The system I've outlined may seem a bit over the top, artificial or drawn out. It does take a lot of time and energy, but it's the best way to achieve your goals and not waste all your efforts. It can help you distil information and make you feel like you are making progress. You also need this system to sort out the good conversations and advice from the less useful coffee meetings. As a former lawyer, keeping written records and paying attention to detail are part of my DNA, so the slightly obsessive spreadsheet process worked well for me. Having now proven it to be successful, I honestly believe it will work well for you too.

Having a proven system makes the networking process easier for you. You don't have to gird your loins for each meeting, work out what questions you should ask and make sure you don't forget really important things.

If you don't feel comfortable with some aspects of the system, feel free to alter them to suit yourself. You will no doubt have some different aspects you wish to capture, or to reflect on using your own individual emphasis.

Make the switch

Set up an Excel spreadsheet, or equivalent, to guide your networking record system. Have a look at the template and set yourself targets – for me, it was five coffee meetings a week, and at least two. Make sure your contacts cover different areas of the NFP sector, if you're not sure of your passion – but make sure you keep your own passions front of mind. My wife kept asking me if I had met with a CEO I mentioned who worked with guide dogs.

She thought it would be lovely for us to have a guide dog at home! I told her I didn't think animals were quite right for me!

Although some preparation is important, don't waste too much time gathering information before starting a networking drive. Balance is vital here. Some preparation is important – but don't let it become an excuse for procrastination.

Ask someone else to help you with your networking. A trusted friend or colleague, or a professional career coach, can sometimes help when you're struggling to break through the inertia. My coach was a great person to have on my side. When I hit the inevitable roadblocks or was struggling to push on, having someone there to put in a supportive word and to remind me of the end goal made all the difference.

Can you picture yourself in your dream role? I used to imagine myself as CEO of a small team, helping young people who were struggling in life. Your actions need to nourish you and give you the motivation and incentive to keep going. Because sometimes, let's face it, it can be really tough.

THE ADVANTAGES OF BEING A CLEANSKIN

People are very open to meeting with a cleanskin – that is, as mentioned earlier, someone who is new to the sector and not aligned to a particular organisation. A cleanskin simply wants any thoughts or expert advice that their NFP contact may have on how to transition to the sector. Being a cleanskin helps you to maximise your chances of the person agreeing to meet with you and being very frank and open in their advice.

NFP leaders are very busy people and may not have much spare time to meet, especially with someone working at a rival charity. But their response seems different if you're a cleanskin. If you have no baggage or potential conflicts, and few connections, people are generally happy to meet with you.

It's a people-centric sector and they like helping someone who's curious and enthusiastic to make a community contribution. By comparison, I had less success with some people I reached out to a second time, after I had been in the NFP sector for several years. Whether it was because I was working for another organisation in their sector or they were busy and felt they'd given me all the advice they had, making times to meet was harder with those people the second time round. Maybe they didn't want to give a hand up to a rival organisation that was chasing the same funds.

If you have no baggage or potential conflicts, and few connections, people are generally happy to meet with you.

Why would a busy NFP executive want to meet with a cleanskin in the first place? It might seem surprising, but they generally do. The strength of the relationship they, or you, have with the referrer can also be a factor. For me, their generosity in being willing to meet became just part of the collaborative and caring culture of the NFP sector. It's also self-perpetuating – because people were so generous with their time when I began my transition, I'm now more than happy to have a coffee with others as they consider switching.

Make the switch

As you become less of a cleanskin and learn more about the sector, some people may no longer want to spend time with you. So just meet with who is available. You'll find that your questions can move to a deeper level as your journey progresses.

WRAP UP

You now understand the importance of networking, developing your own system and sticking to it, the three benefits of networking and the three basic questions. You need to fight inertia by using the system, writing stuff down as you meet people, and picking a few people to ask for initial introductions

118

to their NFP contacts. The system makes it easy and helps you avoid getting stuck. Once you have your system in place, including your target numbers for each week and your three questions, get to work.

In the following chapter, I put together everything you've learned in the preceding chapters, as you get your foot in the door and land your very first gig.

NINE

Putting it all together

Having done all the preparatory work in this book, how do you now bring everything you've learned all together to get your foot in the door and get that elusive first role?

By this stage of the book, you've likely decided you would like to get a not-for-profit (NFP) gig. While your hard work so far has given you a better understanding of the NFP sector and what sort of role might be the right one for you, it's important that you now finish the work by actually getting the job. You deserve a job with fun and meaning, and you don't want to waste all your hard work.

In this chapter, I put together the four areas covered in chapters 4 to 7 and how they relate to getting that first role. I then discuss how to offer yourself for skilled volunteering, if you decide this is your preference. Finally, I outline why you should be flexible with the terms of employment you ask for.

The good news is the NFP sector offers a lot of employment opportunities. According to the Australian Charities and Not-for-Profits Commission's (ACNC's) Australian Charities Report 2018, over 1.3 million people work in the sector – one in ten of Australia's employees. So there should be a role just waiting for you!

FOUR PIECES INTERSECTING

Put together the four main pieces discussed in chapters 4 to 7 – what you like doing, your transferable skills, the cause you're passionate about and working how you want to work. Where do they intersect?

A lovely quote (often misattributed to Aristotle) is, 'Where your talents and the needs of the world cross, there lies your vocation.'

This confluence of your four main pieces seems to have some similarities to the Japanese concept of *ikigai*, which refers to the way a person's satisfaction can be increased through having a direction or purpose in life – through doing what you love, what the world needs, what you are good at and what you can be paid for. This concept is shown in the following figure.

Finding your *ikigai*

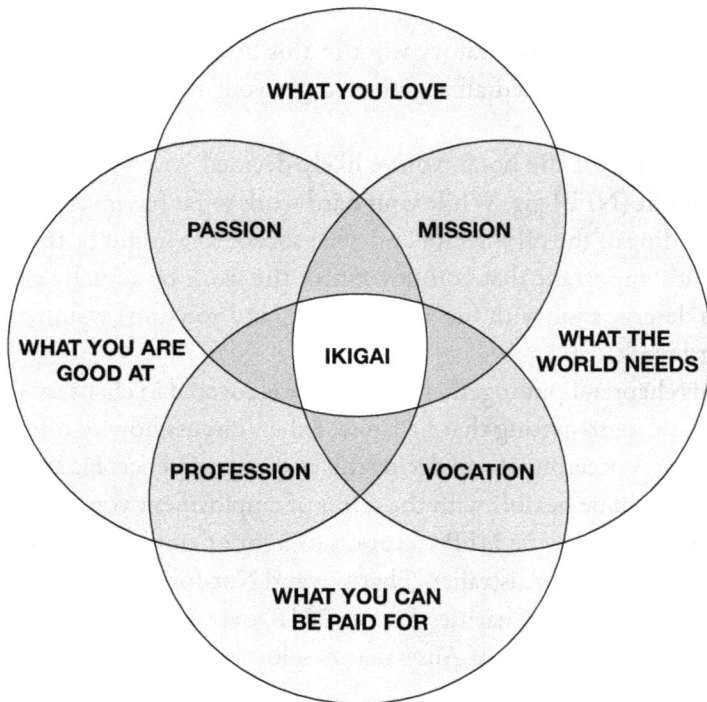

The next step is to brainstorm three potential roles at that intersection. What work and what roles might satisfy the four pieces? Redraft your CV to highlight your transferable skills and your relevant experience. Then go to your network, your key mentors and family and friends to fine-tune and prioritise those three potential roles. Which of them works best for you? I used this method and it was really powerful.

This is where you draw the connection between your old world and your proposed new one – similar to a travel adapter that enables your Aussie plug to fit into a two-pin European socket – and explain

> *Explain to your potential new employers and colleagues in the NFP sector how your previous years of corporate work have equipped you with exactly the right mix of skills and experience to help them achieve their organisation's charitable mission.*

to your potential new employers and colleagues in the NFP sector how your previous years of corporate work have equipped you with exactly the right mix of skills and experience to help them achieve their organisation's charitable mission.

By this stage of my journey, I realised that I liked leading teams that were working in the field with clients – rather than, say, an advocacy role. I had transferable skills from my corporate life that NFP colleagues had told me would be useful. I'd done my newspaper test and that had drawn me to helping young people facing disadvantage. I wanted a job that was more flexible and less demanding than the 60-plus hours I'd worked in the past.

My CV, which for the previous three decades had been used to win legal work, now had to be redrafted for a completely different purpose and audience. My previous emphasis on the areas of law where I had expertise, and the numerous merger and acquisition deals that I'd done, was no longer relevant. In my new draft, I highlighted those aspects of my work history that demonstrated the transferable skills my coffee due diligence and research had told me would be important for the NFP sector. As I've mentioned, I also established a LinkedIn account with a profile that mirrored my revised CV.

Speaking with one of my mentors, I asked whether I could realistically pursue a role as an NFP CEO, given that I had never actually been one. Their suggestion was to tackle the issue head-on and with confidence, by saying something like, 'I am confident that I could be the CEO of an NFP – but I realise that people may focus on my management experience being in a law firm.' By dealing upfront with the elephant in the room, I could then move to a discussion about my skills and passion, and why they made me their ideal candidate.

Brainstorming with my career coach to bring together the four pieces led to three potential roles to explore: CEO of a small- or medium-sized NFP in Australia; senior executive of a large NFP whether in Australia or overseas; or general counsel in an organisation doing good, whether NFP or corporate.

I test-drove those three roles with my network and it became clear that either CEO of a smaller NFP or senior executive of a larger one was the most likely fit. I'd had enough of the law.

This process requires you to revert back to your key coffee mentors for a second meeting now that you have done all that preliminary work. But you should be okay in getting some further advice from them and having them come along with you on the journey. They'll be especially willing if you impressed them with your enthusiasm and commitment at the first meeting, you showed appropriate gratitude at the time, and you've kept in touch (as discussed in the previous chapter, which covers using your networking system). I cannot emphasise enough the truth in the old saying, 'Ask for a job and you'll get advice; ask for advice and you'll get a job'.

The beauty of this process is that by having three roles to test-drive, you can leave in the mix something you're not quite ready to discard – for example, my option of being a general counsel.

On the other hand, if it's clear from all your work that one role would be perfect for you, go ahead and chase that one with all your energy.

Make the switch

Before you start looking for actual roles in the workplace, ask for advice from your network (including family and friends) about specific positions that you think might suit you. Take the time to write down the four pieces you're trying to bring together and a few ideal roles to explore.

GETTING THE RIGHT FIRST ROLE

Although it will depend on what opportunities happen to be around at the time you are looking and on your perceived value in the sector, getting the right first role is important. Aim too low and you'll be tarred with that brush and people will think you want to be a middle manager – even when they believe you could have been CEO. Aim too high and you're likely to find disappointment, not meet expectations and bruise your own reputation for the future. It's a matter of trying to find the right level for you to enter.

I found the right level – one that was not too high for my abilities, nor too low for my expectations. I started as the chief operating officer, the 2IC, in a medium-sized NFP. I learnt a lot, not least about how an NFP CEO and board interact. Although I had spent years advising CEOs and boards at a high level in the corporate world, for the reasons discussed in chapter 2, this experience was very different. Having exposure to the board, and building relationships with individual directors, was a great experience. Several of them said that they could see me in a CEO role in the not too distant future, which really boosted my confidence.

Some people are super-keen to work close to the coal face. Others are happy to support the cause, even if they never have contact with the people their organisation supports. Some people aren't fussed about money. Others need a reasonable salary. And maybe they want a senior role. You need to clarify where you stand on these issues. And talking to your growing NFP network will help you to do so.

Would you like to be the person running the organisation that delivers outdoor programs for young people? Or would you rather be the person who's taking the young people out on the outdoor adventures? Think about where you want to be.

You may be saying to yourself, 'Of course I'm going to get a CEO job.' Or maybe you're saying, 'I don't want to start at the bottom and work my way up. I've done that already in the corporate world.' That approach will not work – but listening and learning with humility will. You might have to accept a lesser or lower-paid role than you had expected.

In my own case, I was keen to find a CEO role – but it took a couple of steps to get there. In each of my roles, the common thread has been helping Australians who are facing disadvantage (that is, people who have fallen through the cracks). But each career step has had a slightly different nuance in that overarching cause – Whitelion focuses on youth at risk, Save the Children on protecting children and supporting their families, Doxa on young people facing socioeconomic disadvantage, Thrive by Five on assisting children and their families in the early years, and SecondBite on feeding hungry Australians (as well as minimising landfill).

Having thought about your ideal first role and salary needs, my advice would be to keep an open mind to any job offer you receive. I'm not saying to be desperate and accept any role But I am saying that switching isn't easy – so be open to the possibility of accepting a lower role or lower salary, and working your way up from there. On the other hand, be careful not to lower external expectations of your value too much. It's a difficult balance.

As one mentor said to me, 'You don't want to be spending your day licking stamps.' I was too impatient and I knew that I wanted a senior executive or CEO role. On the flip side, I remember another mentor telling me, 'Make sure you go somewhere where you're adding value, where there's a problem, where there's difficulties. Don't just get a senior job because it's offered to you.' This ties in with how you can best make your contribution.

Even if you're keen to make a big difference, choosing the right job for you isn't just about the size of the organisation. You also need to consider what impact you can make – with your particular skills and passion. How can you bring in your skills and make a difference?

You may end up making more of a difference in a small organisation than by being a small cog buried behind a laptop in a large one. It's a very personal question.

The attitude of the organisation's leadership and HR team to hiring ex-corporates is one important aspect of your job hunting that you can't control. An openness to employing switchers will obviously work in your favour, particularly if a successful track record has been established by those who have gone before you. But even if (as is usually the case) no history existed of hiring ex-corporates, you can now do the work to be the trailblazer. Good luck!

Even if you're keen to make a big difference, choosing the right job for you isn't just about the size of the organisation. You also need to consider what impact you can make – with your particular skills and passion.

Make the switch

Once you've done the work and know what kind of role you are looking for, make sure you tell your mentor group, so they can keep their eyes and ears open for you.

Look at the NFP job websites to see what roles are out there – for example:

- ethicaljobs.com.au

- probonoaustralia.com.au/jobs

- seek.com.au

- websites of NFPs that appeal to you as prospective employers.

Once you've looked at those websites and found a role that might be right for you, rather than just lodging an application, first make contact to obtain more detail about the role and the way it fits in the organisation. You can gradually build up your sector knowledge that way too.

SKILLED VOLUNTEERING

You may be offered a suitable job from your own network or after applying for a role you saw advertised, and that's great. Snap it up. But it's more likely you'll be waiting for a while for that to happen, which is where skilled volunteering becomes key. In my case, I did some of the preparatory work quietly while I was still working in the corporate world. But I completed most of the work after I'd left my corporate gig, when I had the time and headspace to properly pursue the process I've outlined through this book.

Offering your services for free to your target NFPs is a great way for both parties to get to know each other, and it can often lead to a paid job. Most NFPs have limited resources, so this approach provides a low-risk method for them to get assistance without paying for it – and they can see you have the passion, skills and attitude that would enable you to fit into the organisation. At the same time, you get your foot in the door, giving you a better understanding of how the organisation ticks and where its needs are.

This is the process I used to get my first paid role in the NFP sector. I also used skilled volunteering later on to get a job, even after I had worked in the sector for a while. It's a great strategy to have in your toolkit. When I had finished my research and knew I'd like to work with young people facing disadvantage, I offered my services to a number of organisations working for that cause. The Australian charity sector has 3.7 million volunteers working in it, so hopefully the right opportunity is waiting there just for you!

Offering your services for free to your target NFPs is a great way for both parties to get to know each other, and it can often lead to a paid job.

At my first meeting with Save the Children's Paul Ronalds, he suggested doing project work as a way of clarifying my passions. It also helps to build NFP credibility and relationships.

I also spoke with Whitelion's Mark Watt, and he said, 'We'd love you to sit in on our national monthly executive committee calls.' So, as I mentioned in chapter 5, each month I would dial in and, when the state managers around the country were discussing various issues, I'd try to come up with ideas. I was just there to throw in comments, strategy options and thoughts based on my corporate experience. Once I had shown I could add value, they invited me back for their annual national conference.

Two days before that national conference, the CEO contacted me and said, 'Our chief operating officer's just resigned. He has a young family and doesn't want to travel so much. We've seen your work, would you like the gig?' I was very excited. I spoke with my wife, met with Whitelion's chair – and then signed up straight afterwards.

So that was my first role in the NFP sector – as chief operating officer, and second in command, at a national charity working with youth at risk. My dream had come true!

Looking back, it's not surprising that the first paid gig I got was with an organisation where I had provided skilled volunteering and had also been involved with as a supporter back in my corporate life. As one mentor had said, 'The change you are seeking may be closer than you think.'

Despite all your preparation to get to this stage, you may have some residual doubts about switching. If so, go back to your CV and remind yourself how useful someone with all the skills you've developed over the years could be to an NFP. It's time to talk yourself up, to pump up your own tyres.

If you get an offer to provide skilled volunteering but it's not the kind of offer you'd hoped for – maybe it's too menial, or not using your particular skills – my advice would be to not look a gift horse in the mouth. Say yes and get inside the door. It's only a volunteering role, not a contract. Once you've got your foot in the door, who knows what might happen? A paid role might eventuate.

It might take a while for anything to come up. You might get disheartened after all your hard work. I did. I leaned heavily on my career coach at this stage, especially when I didn't feel like continuing to engage with my network – no more coffees, please. Seek support from those in your network who have made it clear that they're on your team and want to see you switch successfully.

Back in the corporate world, maintaining regular contact with clients was a key part of maintaining my workflow – and some similarities can be seen in the context of your NFP network. You need to keep in touch to be front of mind. As a lawyer, I would find a reason to email and/or call a client regularly – perhaps to let them know of some legal development that might impact them, or to ask how a particular acquisition was performing. They would often say either on the call or in the days soon afterwards, 'Oh, it's good that you called, Steve. I was just thinking of contacting you about a proposal we've started working on.' And off you go, you've won a new client assignment.

To get a job in the NFP world, you need to use the same ongoing discipline and effort.

In her *Harvard Business Review* article 'How to stay stuck in the wrong career', Herminia Ibarra wrote,

> Most of us know what we are trying to escape: the lockstep of a narrowly defined career, inauthentic or unstimulating work, numbing corporate politics, a lack of time for life outside of work. Finding an alternative that truly fits, like finding one's mission in life, cannot be accomplished overnight. It takes time, perseverance and hard work.

So true.

As someone once said, you have to kiss a lot of frogs to find the handsome prince. It's the same in the business world and the NFP world. So keep at it.

Make the switch

Let your key mentors know that you're available. Hopefully some or all of them will be connected with an organisation looking to fill a role that would suit you. I told my mentors, 'I'm now in the market, with a heavily reduced rate down from $800 per hour to

$0 per hour.' It was a cheeky way to encourage them to take up a free resource.

Ask your contacts if they have any current or pending projects that you might be able to help with. Also keep an eye on the job ads, because you might see evidence within them of an organisation's need in a particular area. As well as the employment websites, look at the websites of organisations that match your cause, as many of them advertise vacant positions.

Once you have a skilled volunteering role, keep your eyes open for a paid role in that organisation, or in another organisation working in a similar sort of area – because you now have something on your CV. Working from inside the organisation is a huge advantage when chasing a paid job.

As you look at organisations that make you an offer for skilled volunteering or, ideally, a paid role, my career coach Bill Cowan suggests asking a couple of questions:

- Are your values aligned?

- Can you make a big difference and will they let you do that?

- Where does the role lead?

- Does this fit in with your personal/family life? Think about the hours and the location.

- Will they pay you enough? Your decision is not just about money, but it's a question you need to ask.

Based on Bill's advice to me, here are some questions that you might expect the organisation to ask you:

- Can the organisation trust you?

- Can you do the job? What will it look like in one to five years?

- Do you fit with the organisation?

- Are you enthusiastic?

- Does the organisation look good when they announce you are stepping into that role? Will it impress donors and foundations responsible for funding?

CULTURAL FIT AND FLEXIBILITY

Not all organisations have only one agenda or one cause. Faith-based organisations might have a primary goal to help children in poverty and a secondary goal to, for example, spread the word about their particular religion. You need to look more deeply at the organisation as you get further into research. Make sure that whatever organisation you do choose to support your cause aligns with your deeply held values.

Make sure that whatever organisation you do choose to support your cause aligns with your deeply held values.

Try to learn as much as you can from present and past staff members about the organisation's culture, to ensure it is the right fit for your own values.

As Peter Drucker wrote in 'Managing Oneself' *(Harvard Business Review):*

To work in an organisation whose value system is unacceptable or incompatible with one's own condemns a person both to frustration and to non performance.

You might be surprised to hear that unacceptable value systems exist in organisations established to do good – but unfortunately it does happen.

The other thing to look out for when you're looking at the right fit is evidence of 'founder syndrome'. I've come across this in the NFP sector. I was lucky enough to win a scholarship to travel with some other NFP CEOs to Stanford University and was fascinated to learn there that founder syndrome is also a big issue in NFPs, not just in corporate start-ups. Founder syndrome is where a founder has started an organisation that's done well, and grown to a certain size and maturity where the founder should probably hand it over to someone else to lead. But they don't do so, and it can hold the organisation back.

As noted in Wikipedia, an organisation suffering from founder syndrome is usually strongly identified with the founder, and as a result can be believed to be related to the founder's ego. Instead of meaningful strategy development and shared executive agreement on objectives, there is autocratic and crisis-mode decision-making, micromanagement and no leadership succession planning.

In their *Harvard Business Review* article 'Dealing with a famous founder', authors Marion McCollom Hampton and Ben Francois point out that having an iconic founder is not always a good thing for the sustained health of an organisation. When founders become larger-than-life personas synonymous with their organisation, they begin to overshadow everyone and everything around them. Worse, they can come to believe their own hype and hold next-generation leaders to impossible standards.

A classic example of the opposite of founder syndrome, which they mentioned at Stanford, is Microsoft, where Bill Gates took the organisation from a garage to the multibillion-dollar organisation it is today. That, sadly, doesn't always happen with founders.

FLEXIBLE EMPLOYMENT TERMS

In the corporate world, where you have an established track record and stellar reputation, you may have played hardball in past employment negotiations, making sure that you got the best conditions and weren't paid a cent less than you deserved. That's not the case here. You're taking the road less travelled and so you want to make it as easy as possible for the person offering you a position.

A flexible approach increases the chance of you getting a paid job. If you're not flexible or you're a bit greedy, you might find you miss out.

With the Whitelion chief operating officer role, I was offered a full-time role for a specified salary. But at the same time, I was aware that the organisation had limited resources. I felt I could help if I did the job but at a lesser cost. As a lawyer, I was used to working super efficiently towards tight deadlines to achieve difficult outcomes. So I offered to take less pay, but to work a four-day week – which suited the CEO, the board and me. At Save the Children, I worked a nine-day fortnight. At Doxa, I offered to take less pay, but to have some extra annual leave. This shows how flexibility can work in your favour – helping the charity to save money, but at the same time helping you to find the work–life balance that might be important to you at this stage of your career, leaving time to do other things in life.

A flexible approach increases the chance of you getting a paid job. If you're not flexible or you're a bit greedy, you might find you miss out.

Be careful that your flexible approach is not abused or taken advantage of by a prospective employer. You need to make sure that you are fairly paid for what you are doing. In the NFP sector, the hard and fast rules that might apply in the corporate sector – for example, that you'd be crazy to take a certain sort of role below a certain rate of pay – don't necessarily apply when you're trying to switch. But you have to find a balance between accepting low pay and feeling enthusiastic about taking the job. If you're not getting paid enough and feel like you're being ripped off, you're not going to jump out of bed in the morning. At the same time, you're not doing this for the money that you used to get in the corporate world.

Bear in mind that I'm now talking about senior leadership roles where there are no award rates. A great deal of variety exists in salaries, which leaves it open for you to negotiate an arrangement that suits your personal circumstances.

This is also a great opportunity to display the sector understanding you have developed from all your work to date. If your prospective employer is wary of what expectations you may bring from your old world, you can reassure them that extensive support services and a large corner office are not part of them!

Make the switch

Let potential employers know that you're very flexible regarding salary, hours, working from home and so on. You can hint at it in your application and then say it more directly on first contact or in the interview stage. Maintain flexibility and look for win–wins when that first offer comes in.

It might be an adjustment if you've been used to working for a high corporate salary. Despite your preparation and financial planning, you might find it difficult to accept that your pay packet is less than it has been, perhaps for years. So, expect to take a bit of time to adjust. When you do have those moments, just remind yourself of the difference you're making now with the community, compared to what you were doing before.

I hope that, like me, you prefer your new rich life to your old life of riches.

WRAP UP

You've learned how to put together all your hard work from chapters 4 through 7 to get your first NFP role.

This stage of the process can be a tough one because, unlike the previous stages, you're relying on others to a large extent in order to take action or make a decision. But you don't need to bear that load alone. Your newly minted coffee buddies are now there to support you. So be patient – damaging your brand by rushing into the wrong role is pointless.

Bring together those four pieces of the puzzle and then brainstorm three potential roles, rewrite your CV and LinkedIn profile and test-drive those three roles with your network. When you've done that, you're ready to offer yourself for skilled volunteering, on the way to securing your first paid role.

Once you've got that first paid role, you want to make sure that you succeed in it and stay on in the sector. The next chapter will help you to survive after switching.

TEN

Surviving after switching

Well done. After all your hard work, you've been appointed to your first not-for-profit (NFP) job. In your corporate life, you learned how to hold down a job for pretty much as long as you wanted. Surely you can just do the same thing in the NFP world in order to survive there as an employee? No. Remember what you learned in chapter 2 about the differences between the NFP sector and the business world? Those differences are important and different techniques are required to succeed in this sector.

You want to succeed in this first role. If you don't, getting another gig will be much harder. You could end up fighting against comments like, 'Shame it didn't work out, but you corporate types don't really understand what we're about.'

I've had several rewarding roles since leaving the corporate sector, using the tips I share with you through this chapter.

I start this chapter with a review of the sector differences, before discussing the importance of maintaining your corporate networks. Finally – in the section 'Physician, heal thyself' – I cover looking after people in the NFP sector, including your team and yourself.

SECTOR DIFFERENCES

Remember the differences I discussed in chapter 2? It's important to review and remember them now that you're working with, or leading, staff in the NFP sector. Let your passion show through, listen more than you talk and show humility. Learn about the roles of your staff members, their programs and their challenges. If you're in a leadership role, share your vision and be open to feedback that may change it. Try to suppress your corporate competitive side and strive to be collaborative, but don't leave your corporate background at the door. Use whatever skills and accountability you were employed to deliver. Your role may be largely about changing culture and standards, or setting a new direction. Several of mine have been.

Let your passion show through, listen more than you talk and show humility.

You're less likely to succeed if you don't behave in a way that acknowledges those differences. But failure to bring your corporate background along is also likely to have an adverse impact. You may not deliver what you were employed to achieve.

Not everyone will welcome you to the sector. Steel yourself for the cynics and those who wish you hadn't switched.

People in the NFP sector can think they don't need help from outside or that corporates don't have the right stuff to contribute. Most of the leaders I spoke to could see the need. But sometimes resistance can emerge when you're shoulder to shoulder with someone who's been in the sector for a long time and then you say, 'I'm here to work with you – and I have a suggestion.' I have come across this kind of resistance, particularly from staff who have spent their entire working life in the sector. Cynicism can exist about 'corporate refugees'. Listen to those already in the sector and help them understand that you're on a learning journey yourself. These new colleagues may not have been to university or had the same background that you've had, but they have a lot to teach you. Being humble helps as you make this transition.

Be open-minded and curious. Ask questions. Be determined and patient about your intention to switch. Let everyone know you're in for the long term, because that's what they value. Find supporters within the sector who see your value and can help you maintain your resolve to succeed in the sector – while sometimes also working as your interpreter with existing people in the sector. My mentors could see my passion and enthusiasm, even though I was very green about the sector, and would speak to others and say, 'Please spend some time with Steve. He's the right person and we want him in the sector even though you may not have been interested in talking to him at first.'

You may doubt that the sector differences are so important. Why can't you just perform your job description to the best of your ability, just as you always have? From time to time, you might find yourself reverting to type, behaving as you would in the hard-nosed corporate world – acting along the lines of, 'We'll do it that way because I said so, I'm the boss.' When that happens, take a moment to reflect on the differ-

> *Be open-minded and curious. Ask questions. Be determined and patient about your intention to switch. Let everyone know you're in for the long term, because that's what they value.*

ences covered through this book and how your success in this different sector requires you to do things differently. If you have upset a colleague, an acknowledgement and apology usually helps. Say something like, 'Whoops, sorry about that. That was my old corporate self. Can we rewind please?' Backing off shouldn't be too hard if you've truly approached this transition with humility and an openness to learning.

Make the switch

Review the list of sector differences provided in chapter 2. For each one, assign a specific action as to how you can address that difference in your new role.

MAINTAIN YOUR CORPORATE NETWORKS

Business world issues can be relevant in the NFP world. For example, just like your former colleagues in the business world, you need to understand the regulations in areas such as privacy, and work health and safety. Keeping in contact and maintaining an interest in your old corporate world is good for exercising your mind, especially when staying current with developments in the business sector. It's also good for potential funding, partnerships and other corporate support (such as pro bono professional advice), for mutual benefit.

Keeping up with those corporate networks has helped me in every NFP organisation I've worked with. At Save the Children, I could get support for pro bono legal advice from some of the lawyers I kept in touch with. At Doxa, the corporate world provided job opportunities for our young cadets. At Whitelion, we had a Bailout fundraiser every year where corporates would get locked up in the Old Melbourne Gaol and other similar places around the country. I had great corporate support for that fundraiser. One year, I was proud that 10 per cent of the total funds raised by the event were from my corporate connections. At SecondBite, my corporate network led to valuable partnerships, funding and even a full-blown (and free) strategic review of our warehouses around the country.

Some colleagues in the corporate world will, of course, be happy to stay working there but may want, as I did, opportunities to give back to the community. They can feel much more comfortable about getting involved when they're dealing with somebody from their own world. With most people in the corporate world, you can strike a chord if you've got the right cause and passion. They want to help and they are relieved when they find someone who is passionate and who can say, 'I understand where you're at. You're doing great work in the corporate world. You're keeping the economy ticking, you're creating jobs. I can help you find a way to help in a different area. It'll be great for your organisation too. I know how corporates work – you'll be able to market your support of our NFP in your staff newsletter and in your staff recruitment. This is a win–win.'

Maybe finding the time to maintain old connections is hard, or maybe you feel you don't have much in common anymore. You could just move on from your corporate past and put 100 per cent of your focus and effort into your new job and sector. But that would be a mistake. It's important to save some of your energy to maintain those business connections and to do so regularly. Using your networking system from chapter 8 will provide a structure to maintain your corporate network, and to diarise reminders to set up meetings with your corporate mentors and supporters. In between those face-to-face meetings, I use emails and phone calls about something of mutual interest to keep connected. Cut and paste (with any required editing) is a wonderful invention when it comes to emails.

Contacting your mentors to seek support after a break of several years is more difficult and perhaps a bit cheeky, but I admit sometimes I did this. Ask them about what's going on in their business and in the business world generally. Most people like to talk about themselves and their work. What issues are they facing? You can then discuss whether those issues will also be relevant to you in your NFP role.

In return, you can tell them about life on the other side. I found many were interested in, if somewhat bemused by, my switching journey. They quizzed me during our regular calls on how it was all going. If you similarly maintain regular contact, you can seek their input and help on the big issues you're facing at the time. For example, I once had to dismiss the manager of one of our interstate offices and act as interim state manager for several months. It was really helpful to talk to someone in my network who had extensive experience running a medium-sized business with direct line responsibility for staff in other locations, and their advice was spot on.

Make the switch

Keep in touch with key corporates throughout your journey, just as you did with customers and clients in your former life. You'll be busy. So use your networking spreadsheet system from chapter 8 to help maintain the necessary self-discipline for meetings to take place regularly.

PHYSICIAN, HEAL THYSELF – LOOKING AFTER YOUR TEAM, INCLUDING YOURSELF AS LEADER

Beware of leadership burnout once you've made the switch. The lack of resources in the NFP sector can lead to a lack of support for leaders. Frontline workers get 'supervision', which has a different meaning in the sector, to help cope with their heavy workloads and stressful client situations – for example, staff working with clients in domestic violence or youth detention. But the leadership group often misses out. As a CEO, I established systems to support the senior executive team and their mental health, and tried to keep close enough to my team to sense when issues were arising. On a lighter note, I always try to celebrate success often – and to have fun! Life is too short not to.

Looking after yourself and your team is something that needs constant attention. The high turnover in the sector may be partly due to these sorts of pressures.

But if you are the CEO, who looks after you and your wellbeing? You need your own support team – for example, your key mentors, CEO support groups and other people you meet at your level along the way.

You need your own support team – for example, your key mentors, CEO support groups and other people you meet at your level along the way.

I meet regularly with the Australian NFP CEOs I met on my scholarship to Stanford University in the US. Similarly, I have received great encouragement over the years from a support group of CEOs from organisations working with young people. Support groups like these can help with your own mental health, in a sector that can sometimes be very draining emotionally.

In one of our organisations, a client committed suicide in a situation that was very tough on the youth worker who was working with that young person. The rest of the team were also deeply affected. We involved counsellors and some time off for the staff member and those close to her. I raised the issue in the youth support CEO network and a number of them had had similar issues in the past. They gave me some excellent advice on how we might deal with the issue, to best assist my team. In these CEO support groups, we can talk confidentially about tough situations, and get some support and feedback, including advice without judgement.

One of the CEO support groups I am in meets every few months. We take turns hosting and providing snacks. We talk about things such as personnel issues, fundraising and dealing with our boards. It can be lonely as an NFP CEO and it's great to have this kind of mutual support system.

Have you ever played the old arcade game Whac-A-Mole? No sooner have you hit one mole down with the hammer, than another one pops up elsewhere on the table. Sometimes being a CEO in the NFP sector can feel like that. You're dealing with staff issues, funding and regulatory concerns, changing the toner in the photocopier, working on the smell of an oily rag. But rather than try to deal with every single issue that arises in your organisation, several of my NFP CEO colleagues said they use the 80/20 rule or a variation of it. By focusing on what you consider to be the most important 20 per cent of the issues, you'll get 80 per cent of the results you're after – and you'll get away from the office before midnight.

It's a marathon, not a sprint. As a refugee from another world, it can be particularly lonely for leaders who have switched. My vision is that one day enough of us will have switched that we'll be able to make up our own support groups!

I've seen the value of my own support groups in helping to share the load when times are tough, and to bounce off ideas when you're resolving a thorny issue – such as how best a CEO can manage their chair or board!

You might be saying, 'If I can survive a tough corporate career, I can cope with whatever the NFP world can throw at me.' A great attitude, but be aware that this is a people-centric sector, working to help those whose situations can be very upsetting. You'll never have enough hours in the day or dollars in the bank to deal with all the people who need and deserve support from you and your organisation. You will experience more highs and lows, and more emotional stress from contact with frontline clients facing disadvantage. You won't have all the facilities, backup staff, IT support, back office staff and the finer things that you used to have. To avoid getting overwhelmed by all those things, look after your team and yourself. The suggestions from this section will help you do that.

Make the switch

Look after your executive team and look after yourself – be aware of your own mental health and wellbeing, practise the 80/20 rule and celebrate regularly. Identify which of your mentors is available to provide that extra support – possibly someone you've known before the switch or maybe one of your new coffee buddies.

You may not realise that you're getting stressed and burned out. You can agree in advance with a friend, mentor or your partner that they're going to tell you when they see that you're hitting a wall. Also agree on an action plan. What are you – with their help – going to do then? Are you going to take some time off? Are you going to see a counsellor? How are you going to deal with that issue? If you can agree to a plan beforehand, you'll already have a way through this stressful situation when you need it.

Setting up support systems such as these will help you through the occasional rocky patch, so you can continue to enjoy the deep satisfaction that comes from purposeful work.

WRAP UP

It's immensely satisfying in the NFP sector, but it's also hard work. Often, fewer resources are available and an unending group of clients need support. But you now have some tips on how to deal with those challenges and succeed in your first NFP role.

One of the best ways to succeed in the sector is to surround yourself with individuals or support groups who can back you up when things are tough. This can be difficult when you're new to the sector. Even if the first person you approach says, 'No, find someone else to ask,' you'll be surprised at how generous people are in helping others in the NFP sector. Especially if you ask while you are still a relative cleanskin, as I discuss in chapter 8.

Make a list of the actions you're going to take, as discussed earlier in this chapter. Establish that system to help you keep in frequent contact with your corporate network, and use the tips provided here to look after your team and yourself.

Well done on achieving the NFP role you were seeking, whether as CEO or as a staff member.

Sometimes I think back to how my father was denied the chance to get everything he wanted from his life. I am so grateful for all he taught me about service to the community – and also for the opportunity to switch to a more purposeful second career.

Switching may be hard work. But it also opens the door to a fulfilling purpose that you may never have dreamed possible. And once you have switched, you also have the tools you need to survive.

Wrapping up

I often reflect on how different my life has been since I sat years ago watching the sun set over that French village – and how pleased I am that I decided to switch sectors.

We only have one life. I hope that by now you've fully considered whether a switch to the NFP sector is the right next step for you. If it is, this step-by-step guide will help you (or has helped you!) find an NFP role that is ideal for you and has the purpose and meaning you want.

Imagine heading off each day to an inspiring role that uses the skills and experience you have built over your time in the corporate sector – instead of dragging yourself off to a job that has lost its meaning and purpose.

Day to day you'll be meeting – and assisting – people from completely different environments to your own. You'll be working with staff from a much broader background than you have before. Each day you will face new challenges – and overcome them. You can make a positive difference and help people less fortunate. What a rewarding way to spend your time.

So move from that comfy chair in your corporate corner office. You may end up in a dingy office on the city fringe, rather than a gleaming skyscraper in the CBD. Reflect on why you want to transition to the NFP sector – discovering that rich life, and the fulfilment of making a difference each day. Ask yourself the four guiding questions to direct your journey. Grow your network so you can learn about the sector. Put together a mentor group to test drive your ideas, to back you when you need help, and to keep you in the loop about upcoming roles.

Use techniques such as skilled volunteering to bring it all together and get your first role. Finally, celebrate that you're living a full life and making a meaningful contribution every day to an important cause.

Leaving behind the security of your corporate life to move to the NFP sector and trying to change the world isn't easy. That's probably why few people (so far) have succeeded in transitioning. But there's no better time than now to take the first step.

I've now told you everything I know to help you succeed in switching. Go for it.

I hope that everyone who no longer finds their work to be fulfilling can find a role that uses their corporate skills and experience to make a meaningful difference in an area they're passionate about. And that, in doing so, we pay forward the good fortune we've had in the corporate sector, by helping to make this world a better place.

Good luck!

Steve Clifford

Acknowledgements

'It takes a village to write a book.'

It seems paradoxical to me that, after having spent more solo time than ever before in my life in a room on my own writing this book, I have so many people to thank for its creation.

Firstly, my book coach Kath Walters, for giving me encouragement when I felt that I had nothing worthwhile to say, and for breaking the task into bite-size pieces through her amazing 90-day process. (Of course, I failed the 90-day deadline miserably, but thanks to Kath's brilliant skills and cheerful perseverance, you have the book in your hands anyway.)

I was introduced to Kath by Leonie Green, whom I mentored at one stage, before Leonie's career took off and she wrote her own wonderful book about leadership.

To my 'first readers', for taking the time to read and critique the manuscript:

- Michael Traill, the iconic pioneer of switching from corporate to NFP land and author of *Jumping Ship*, who has been there for switching advice throughout my journey

- Paul Ronalds, a former boss as CEO of Save the Children Australia, who is also an author and deep thinker about NFPs in the 21st century, as well as being a wonderful mentor and supporter

- Graeme Johnson, a dear friend and mentor from my Allens legal days, who taught me how people should be treated in the workplace, and who has been a chair and director of several NFPs

- Michaela Healey, an ex NAB senior executive who has done her own version of switching, and gave insightful manuscript comments from someone who understands diversity and a 21st-century way of thinking that an older, white male like me sometimes struggles with

- Simon McKeon, who I worked with on big deals in the corporate world and who has been a solid supporter of my switching journey

- old friends Geoff Bennett, Michele Layet (an author herself, with a proofreading superpower), Alan Talbot (also an author), Michael Dixon and John Tilleard, who all know me well enough to ensure that my words were authentic.

A good career coach changes your life, and I have been fortunate enough to have two of them:

- initially when at Allens I met Craig Perrett, and we started painting a picture of my post-corporate life, before becoming great mates

- as I approached the end of my corporate life, I was introduced to Bill Cowan, who is one of the wisest (and best connected) people I know. Many of the ideas in this book are based on what I learnt from Bill.

When I finally finished the book and came to think about publishing it, I received wonderful support from:

- Michael Hanrahan and his team at Publish Central, especially Charlotte Duff (who won my undying gratitude by drafting suggested changes rather than just sending them back to me to do all the work) and Anna Clemann

- dear friend (and best-selling author) Li Cunxin, who gave me great advice on publishing and has been a constant source of encouragement on my switching journey

- Li also introduced me to prolific author Dr John Tickell, who enthusiastically assisted me in understanding the wonderful world of publishing

- sister-in-law Jennifer Hutchison also helped me, using her expertise as an author and publisher

- old friend Nick Barnett, who has written several books and was willing to share many thoughtful insights about what is involved, on top of being a constant supporter on my journey.

Much of the book was written during covid lockdowns, when my Somers friends John Tilleard and Mike Sandiford took me mountain biking and beach walking respectively, to keep my sanity in between writing sessions. They also pretended to know about writing books, offering me gratuitous advice, even when I didn't ask for it and didn't really want it.

All of my colleagues over the last seven years in the NFP sector have taught me so much along the way, as I have lurched from one stuff up to the next, including:

- Mark Watt, founder and former CEO of Whitelion, to whom I will forever be grateful for giving me my first job in the sector

- Elizabeth Mildwater, who switched from corporate life for a while and brought me into Save the Children while she was there

- the executive team at Doxa Youth Foundation, who did a wonderful job changing young lives in that organisation's better days, and who taught their first-time CEO so much about collaborative leadership (including Shona, who would challenge just about every decision I made)

- the CEO support groups that I have been privileged to be part of, such as Jo Swift and the Youth Collaboration Group, as well as Cat Fay and the inspirational 2018 Stanford Perpetual CEO group

- all my other NFP colleagues since 2014. Thank you all.

This book talks about the enormous value that mentors can bring to someone switching to the NFP sector. I have been absolutely blessed with the quality and quantity of my mentors over many decades, not just during switching season. In addition to those named above, and at the risk of offending the many whose names the editor won't let me keep adding (but you know who you are anyway!), I would like to add my sincere gratitude to all of the following kindhearted friends and mentors for their wise counsel over recent years and decades:

Bruce Akhurst, John Allen, Paul Brasher, Catherine Brown, Ian Carson, Leigh Clifford, Laurie Cox, Richard Dent, Sylvie Descamp, Andrew Fairley, Flavia Gobbo, Andrew Hagger, Alice Macdougall, Stephanie Mathieson, Philip Mayers, Lindsay Maxsted, Rachael McLennan, Rupert Myer, Bruce Parncutt, Kathie Sampson, Helen Szoke, Christopher Thorn, Gillian Triggs, Leonard Vary and all my Allens colleagues past and present including Colin Galbraith, Jon Webster, Peter Stewart and Richard Spurio.

To my closest friends and family: Rossco, Hunto and Michael (and Eddo in the US), Tony Orr, my brothers Graeme and Richard, my late parents Bruce and Barbara, my adult kids Amelia, Robert and Simon (and their partners Tom, Harper and Matilda) – all of you have challenged and supported me along the way and for that I will be forever grateful.

And finally to Amanda, my gorgeous wife and life partner. I cherish you and am so grateful for your loving and unconditional support in what I'm doing – even though sometimes you're a bit perplexed as to why I'm doing it!

www.ingramcontent.com/pod-product-compliance
Lightning Source LLC
Chambersburg PA
CBHW071643210326
41597CB00017B/2098